LIVING THE

MISSION

OTHER RENOVARÉ RESOURCES

Connecting with God
by Lynda L. Graybeal and Julia L. Roller

Devotional Classics
co-edited by Richard J. Foster and James Bryan Smith

Embracing the Love of God
by James Bryan Smith

Learning from Jesus
by Lynda L. Graybeal and Julia L. Roller

Prayer and Worship
by Lynda L. Graybeal and Julia L. Roller

The Renovaré Spiritual Formation Bible
edited by Richard J. Foster and others

Songs for Renewal
by Janet Lindeblad Janzen with Richard J. Foster

Spiritual Classics
co-edited by Richard J. Foster and Emilie Griffin

A Spiritual Formation Journal
created by Jana Rea with Richard J. Foster

A Spiritual Formation Workbook
by James Bryan Smith with Lynda L. Graybeal

Streams of Living Water
by Richard J. Foster

Wilderness Time
by Emilie Griffin

✦

OTHER BOOKS
BY RICHARD J. FOSTER

Celebrating the Disciplines
with Kathryn A. Helmers

Celebration of Discipline

The Challenge of the Disciplined Life

Freedom of Simplicity

Prayer: Finding the Heart's True Home

Prayers from the Heart

Richard J. Foster's Study Guide for Celebration of Discipline

Seeking the Kingdom

LIVING THE

MISSION

A SPIRITUAL FORMATION GUIDE

A RENOVARÉ RESOURCE

FOR INDIVIDUALS AND GROUPS

Introduction by Richard J. Foster

Lynda L. Graybeal and Julia L. Roller

HarperOne
An Imprint of HarperCollinsPublishers

HarperOne

For information about RENOVARÉ write to RENOVARÉ, 8 Inverness Dr East, Suite 102, Englewood, CO 80112-5624 USA or log on to the Web site http://www.renovare.org.

HarperCollins books may be purchased for educational, business, or sales promotional use. For information, please e-mail the Special Markets Department, at SPsales@harpercollins.com.

HarperCollins Web site: http://www.harpercollins.com

HarperCollins®, ☕®, and HarperOne™
are trademarks of HarperCollins Publishers.

FIRST EDITION

Designed by Sharon VanLoozenoord

Library of Congress Cataloging-in-Publication Data is available.

ISBN: 978–0–06–084126–3

ISBN-10: 0–06–084126–5

22 23 24 LSC(H) 16 15 14 13 12

CONTENTS

❖

INTRODUCTION

❖

For five years I engaged in what is bound to be my life's richest adventure of biblical work. Five of us (in time to be called general editors) were wrestling with the whole of Scripture through the lens of spiritual formation, seeing what we could learn and how we could be formed and conformed and transformed ever more deeply in the subterranean chambers of the soul. That project eventually came into published form as *The Renovaré Spiritual Formation Bible*.

How do I describe to you the excitement of those early days? To be sure, it was genuine work, for the intensity of labor was exhausting, but it was so much more than "work." It was the thrill of creative ideas flying fast and furious, of dynamic insights crammed one upon another. In those chaotic sessions I often felt like I was astride a wild stallion at full gallop, gripping the mane for dear life.

But it wasn't just the excitement of new concepts emerging out of the wealth of pooled intellectual capital. No, it was the sense of awe before the majesty of Scripture, of being drawn in toward the Divine Center, of holy stillness, of quiet worship and whispered promptings. And prayers—morning prayers and evening prayers and days soaked in prayerful sharing over the sacred text. Oh yes, and laughter. Deep, side-splitting belly laughter. Holy hilarity I guess you could call it.

The experience was joyfully creative and soul-expanding. We knew we were onto something big—big ideas with huge consequences for the hearts and minds of precious people.

At some point in this dynamic process we began to ask if a way could be found to help those who would read this *Renovaré Bible* to experience something of the excitement and adventure we had in first hammering out the concepts of the "Immanuel Principle" and the "with-God life." Could others discover for themselves how the "with-God" framework illuminates God's purposes in history? How over many centuries and through multiple human authors, God has so superintended the development of the Bible that it speaks to us about real life (*zoë*) and teaches us how to live "with God" through the vicissitudes of human experience? How the aim of God in history is the creation of an all-inclusive community of loving persons, with God himself included in this community as its prime sustainer and most glorious inhabitant? How the unity of the Bible is discovered in the lived community reality of this *zoë* life under God and with God and through the power of God?

And so these spiritual formation guides were born. Together they will take us on a journey through the entire panorama of Scripture. Through these spiritual formation guides, we will discover how the Old Testament depicts God's pursuit of loving relationship with his chosen people, Israel, and how through Israel all the peoples of the earth are to be blessed. We see this "pursuit of loving relationship" carried on through the lives of the patriarchs, the history of the Israelites in their exodus from slavery and their entrance into the Promised Land, in the forming and then the disintegration of tribe and nation. Then, the New Testament depicts the story of God's fulfillment of "loving relationship" with a people who become God's own through their identity in Jesus Christ: "God's household, having been built upon the foundation of the apostles and prophets, Christ Jesus Himself being the corner *stone,* in whom the whole building, being fitted together, is growing into a holy temple in the Lord; in whom you also are being built together into a dwelling of God in the Spirit" (Eph 2:19–22, NASB).

As the Bible closes, it opens a window onto the fulfillment of God's purposes for humanity beyond human history: "Now the dwelling of God is with human beings, and he will live with them. They will be his people, and God himself will be with them and be their God" (Rev 21:3, NIVI).

Thus, we will discover that the Immanuel Principle is, after all, a cosmic principle that God has used all along in creation and redemption. It alone serves to guide human life aright on earth now and even illuminates the future of the universe. Of course, the few examples I have shared here hardly touch the surface of the great river of life that flows from God through Scripture and into the thirsty wastelands of the human soul. "Let anyone who is thirsty come to me [Jesus] and drink. Whoever believes in me, as the Scripture has said, will have streams of living water flowing from within" (John 7:37–38, NIVI).

This study guide, therefore, has been created to help each of us enter into the story of the Bible so as to see our own story, our own journey in the great cosmic drama of divine-human relationship. May you, may I, choose to surrender freely to this river of life, receiving and helping others to receive this Life, this *Zoë,* as our own.

Richard J. Foster

HOW TO USE THIS GUIDE

❖

This book is dedicated to nurturing spiritual formation through the study of Scripture. Devotional excerpts from the writings of ancient and contemporary Christians; questions for reflection; and exercises centered around Spiritual Disciplines, such as study, prayer, solitude, meditation, and silence; supplement and illumine the biblical text. This book is not intended to be read passively; it requires the interactive participation of you the reader. To engage with the texts we have chosen and to do the exercises we have set out here will require time and dedication beyond mere reading of the guide. We hope you will accept this challenge!

Whether you are using the guide as an individual or as a group, we recommend that you begin by reading "The With-God Life" and becoming familiar with the accompanying chart, which will give you some insight into the role of Scripture in the process of spiritual formation. Then you should read the Overview, which will give you a sense of the main themes we discuss. The material in the chapters of this guide is intended to help you take the next step—to engage in activities that will help you grow closer to God.

INSTRUCTIONS FOR INDIVIDUALS

Because this book is an interactive guide for spiritual formation, we recommend that you read it more slowly than you would another kind of book. Read the Devotional and Scripture Readings and the My Life with God Exercise at the beginning of each chapter, then try to give yourself at least a week to do the exercise before reading the rest of the chapter. You may want to use a journal or notebook to record your responses to the questions in the chapter. Move on to a new chapter when you feel ready.

INSTRUCTIONS FOR GROUPS

If this is your first time participating in a spiritual formation group, your first question is likely: What *is* a spiritual formation group, anyway? Simply put, a spiritual formation group consists of two to seven people who meet together on a regular basis, bringing challenge and focus to their spiritual lives. Through mutual encouragement and accountability, spiritual formation groups enable their members to assist one another on the road of discipleship to Jesus Christ. We need encouragement during the times when we succeed and the times when we fail in our life of discipleship. We need others to keep us accountable, to remind us to continually pursue our lives with God and our discipleship to Jesus. Each is a natural by-product of the spiritual formation group experience.

If you are just starting a group, try recruiting one or two friends and asking each to recruit one other person. You could also place an ad in your church bulletin or make an announcement at your weekly service. Try to limit your group to seven people or fewer. With a larger group, meetings tend to run too long and not all members participate equally. Four or five people is optimal.

Plan for at least twelve group meetings, each dedicated to a chapter. (You might choose to have an additional introductory meeting or an extra final meeting for evaluation and making future plans.) Meet as often as once a week or as infrequently as once a month, whatever is best for your group. Each meeting should last sixty to ninety minutes. Although you may want to designate someone to be in charge of initial logistics and communication about meeting times and places, we have designed these guides to work in a leaderless format. Each week a different person serves as a facilitator to keep the discussion moving along. No extra study or preparation is required for that person; he or she simply follows the group directions in the margins of each chapter.

Before the first meeting, each member should read the Devotional and Scripture Readings and do the My Life with God Exercise in the first chapter. Because of these requirements and to make group meetings easier, it is helpful for each member of the group to have their own copy of this book. Members read ahead in this way before every meeting. The exercises are quite involved and require a time commitment of at least a few minutes each day over several days. Allow at least a week for members to do the exercise before holding the first meeting. Some may wish to read through the entire chapter beforehand, but it is not necessary to do so.

At the end of each chapter are additional exercises, resources, and reflection questions. These optional sections are primarily intended for individual use after the group meeting. Some may enjoy writing out answers to the reflection questions in the extra space provided or in their journals or notebooks. But if your group is quite interested in a particular chapter, you might consider incorporating the Additional Reflection Questions into your group meeting.

Now you are ready to form your group and plan your first meeting! May God bless you richly in this endeavor.

Lynda L. Graybeal and Julia L. Roller

~ ∽

THE WITH-GOD LIFE

❖

Adapted from an essay in The Renovaré Spiritual Formation Bible *by Gayle Beebe,*
Richard J. Foster, Lynda L. Graybeal, Thomas C. Oden, and Dallas Willard

CATCHING THE VISION: THE LIFE

The Bible is all about human life "with God." It is about how God has made this "with-God" life possible and will bring it to pass. In fact, the name Immanuel, meaning in Hebrew "God is with us," is the title given to the one and only Redeemer because it refers to God's everlasting intent for human life—namely, that we should be in every aspect a dwelling place of God. *Indeed, the unity of the Bible is discovered in the development of life with God as a reality on earth, centered in the person of Jesus.* We might call this the *Immanuel Principle* of life.

This dynamic, pulsating, with-God life is on nearly every page of the Bible. To the point of redundancy, we hear that *God is with* his people: with Abraham and Moses, with Esther and David, with Isaiah, Jeremiah, Amos, Micah, Haggai, and Malachi, with Mary, Peter, James, and John, with Paul and Barnabas, with Priscilla and Aquila, with Lydia, Timothy, Epaphroditus, Phoebe, and with a host of others too numerous to name.

Accordingly, the primary purpose of the Renovaré guides is to enable us to see and understand the reality of the "with-God" life, to enter the process of the transformation of our whole person and of our whole life into *Christlikeness*.

Opening Ourselves to the Life

If we want to receive from the Bible the life "with God" that is portrayed *in* the Bible, we must be prepared to have our dearest and most fundamental assumptions about ourselves and our associations called into question. We must read humbly and in a constant attitude of repentance. Only in this way can we gain a thorough and practical grasp of the spiritual riches that God has made available to all humanity in his written Word.

When we turn to Scripture in this way, our reason for "knowing" the Bible and everything it teaches is that we might love more and know more of love.

We experience this love not as an abstraction but as a practical reality that possesses us. And because all those who love thoroughly obey the law, we would become ever more obedient to Jesus Christ and his Father.

Our goal is not to control the Bible—that is, to try to make it "come out right"—but simply to release its life into our lives and into our world. We seek to trust the living water that flows from Christ through the Bible, to open ourselves to this living water and to release it into the world as best we can, and then get out of its way.

NURTURING THE INTENTION: THE BIBLE

God remains with the Bible always. It is God's book. No one owns it but God himself. It is the loving heart of God made visible and plain. And receiving this message of exquisite love is the great privilege of all who long for life with God. *Reading, studying, memorizing, and meditating upon Scripture has always been the foundation of the Christian disciplines.* All of the disciplines are built upon Scripture. Our practice of the Spiritual Disciplines is kept on course by our immersion in Scripture. And so it is, we come to see, that this reading, studying, memorizing, and meditating is totally in the service of "the life which is life indeed" (1 Tim 6:19, RSV). We long with all our heart to know *for ourselves* this with-God kind of life that Jesus brings in all its fullness.

And the Bible has been given to help us. God has so superintended the writing of Scripture that it serves as a most reliable guide for our spiritual formation. But God uses human action in its presentation to the world, just as it is authored by humans. Thus we must consider how we ourselves can come to the Bible and also how we can present it to all peoples in a way that inducts the soul into the eternal kind of life.

We begin by finding experientially, day by day, how to let Jesus Christ live in every dimension of our being. In Christian community, we can open our lives to God's life by gathering regularly in little groups of two or more to encourage one another to discover the footprints of God in our daily existence and to venture out *with God* into areas where we have previously walked alone or not at all.

But the aim is not external conformity, whether to doctrine or deed, but the re-formation of the inner self—of the spiritual core, the place of thought and feeling, of will and character. The psalmist cries, "You desire truth in the inward being; therefore teach me wisdom in my secret heart.... Create in me a clean heart, O God, and put a new and right spirit within me" (Ps 51:6, 10). It is the "inner person" that is being "*renewed [renovaré] day by day*" (2 Cor 4:16, emphasis added).

While the many Christian traditions differ over the details of spiritual formation, they all come out at the same place: the transformation of the person into Christlikeness. "Spiritual formation" is the process of transforming the inner reality of the self (the *inward being* of the psalmist) in such a way that the overall life with God seen in the Bible naturally and freely comes to pass in us. Our inner world (the *secret heart*) becomes the home of Jesus, by his initiative and our response. As a result, our interior world becomes increasingly like the inner self of Jesus and, therefore, the natural source of words and deeds that are characteristic of him. By his enabling presence, we come to "let the same mind be in you that was in Christ Jesus" (Phil 2:5).

UNDERSTANDING THE MEANS:
THE SPIRITUAL DISCIPLINES

This "with-God" life we find in the Bible is the very life to which we are called. In fact, it is exactly the life Jesus is referring to when he declares, "I am come that they might have life, and that they might have *it* more abundantly" (John 10:10, KJV). It is a life of unhurried peace and power. It is solid. It is serene. It is simple. It is radiant. It takes no time, though it permeates all of our time.

But such a life does not simply fall into our hands. Frankly, it is no more automatic for us than it was for those luminaries who walk across the pages of the Bible. There is a God-ordained way to become the kind of people and communities that can fully and joyfully enter into such abundant living. And this involves intentionally "train[ing] ... in godliness" (1 Tim 4:7). This is the purpose of the *disciplines* of the spiritual life. Indeed, the very reason for these spiritual formation guides is so that Scripture may be the primary means for the discovery, instruction, and practice of the Spiritual Disciplines, which bring us all the more fully into the with-God life.

The Spiritual Disciplines, then, are the God-ordained means by which each of us is enabled to bring the little, individualized power-pack we all possess—we call it the human body—and place it before God as "a living sacrifice" (Rom 12:1). It is the way we go about training in the spiritual life. By means of this process we become, through time and experience, the kind of person who naturally and freely expresses "love, joy, peace, patience, kindness, generosity, faithfulness, gentleness, and self-control" (Gal 5:22–23).

Many and Varied

What are these Spiritual Disciplines? They include fasting and prayer, study and service, submission and solitude, confession and worship, meditation and silence, simplicity, frugality, secrecy, sacrifice, and celebration. Such Spiritual Disciplines crop up repeatedly in the Bible as the way God's people trained themselves and were trained by God to achieve godliness. And not only in the Bible: the saints down through history, and even spilling over into our own time, have all practiced these ways of "grow[ing] in grace" (2 Pet 3:18).

A Spiritual Discipline is an intentionally directed action by which we do what we *can* do in order to receive from God the ability (or power) to do what we cannot achieve by direct effort. It is not in us, for example, to love our enemies. We might try very hard to love our enemies, but we will fail miserably. Always. This strength, this power to love our enemies—that is, to genuinely and unconditionally love those who curse us and spitefully use us—is simply not within our natural abilities. We cannot do it by ourselves. Ever.

But this *fact of life* does not mean that we do nothing. Far from it! Instead, by an act of the will we choose to take up disciplines of the spiritual life that we can do. These disciplines are all actions of body, mind, and spirit that are within our power. Not always and not perfectly, to be sure. But they are things we can do. By choice. By choosing actions of *fasting, study, solitude,* and so forth.

Their Purpose

The Spiritual Disciplines in and of themselves have no merit whatsoever. They possess no righteousness, contain no rectitude. Their purpose—their only purpose—is to place us before God. After that they have come to the end of their usefulness. But it is enough. Then the grace of God steps in and takes this simple offering of ourselves and creates out of it a person who embodies the goodness of God—indeed, a person who can come to the place of truly loving even enemies.

Again, Spiritual Disciplines involve doing what we *can* do to receive from God the power to do what we cannot do. And God graciously uses this process to produce in us the kind of person who automatically will do what needs to be done when it needs to be done.

Now, this ability to do what needs to be done when it needs to be done is the true freedom in life. Freedom comes not from the absence of restraint but from the presence of discipline. When we are on the spot, when we find ourselves in the midst of a crisis, it is too late. Training in the Spiritual Disciplines is the God-ordained means for forming and transforming the human personality so that when we are in a crisis we can be "response-able"—able to respond appropriately.

EXPERIENCING THE GRACE OF GOD: THE EFFORT

It is vitally important for us to see all this spiritual training in the context of the work and action of God's grace. As the great apostle Paul reminds us, "It is God who is at work in you, enabling you both to will and to work for his good pleasure" (Phil 2:13). This, you see, is no "works righteousness," as it is sometimes called. Even our desire for this "with-God" kind of life is an action of grace; it is "prevenient grace," as the theologians say. You see, we are not just saved by grace, we live by grace. We pray by grace and fast by grace and study by grace and serve by grace and worship by grace. *All the disciplines are permeated by the enabling grace of God.*

But do not misunderstand—there *are* things for us to do. Daily. Grace never means inaction or total passivity. In ordinary life we will encounter many moments of decision when we must engage the will, saying "Yes!" to God's will and to God's way, as the People of God have done throughout history.

The opposite of grace is works, not effort. "Works" have to do with earning, and there simply is nothing any of us can do to earn God's love or acceptance. And, of course, we don't have to. God already loves us utterly and perfectly, and our complete acceptance is the free gift of God through Jesus Christ our Lord. In God's amazing grace, we live and move and have our being. But if we ever hope to "grow in grace," we will find ourselves engaging in effort of the most strenuous kind. As Jesus says, we are to "*strive* to enter through the narrow door" (Luke 13:24, emphasis added). And Peter urges us to "make every *effort* to support your faith with goodness, and goodness with knowledge, and knowledge with self-control, and self-control with endurance, and endurance with godliness, and godliness with mutual affection, and mutual affection with love" (2 Pet 1:5–7, emphasis added). It is this formation—indeed transformation—that we all desire.

TRAVELING WITH THE PEOPLE OF GOD: THE JOURNEY

The luminaries who walk across the pages of our Bible not only practiced the various and sundry Spiritual Disciplines that formed—indeed transformed—them into Christlikeness, but did so while on a journey. The Bible records their lives as they traveled from the Garden of Eden to Canaan to Egypt to the Promised Land to Babylon and back. Then Jesus instructed the People of God to be his witnesses "to the ends of the earth" (Acts 1:8c), until they arrive at their final destination, "a new heaven and new earth" (Rev 21:1). During their travels God made himself known in various ways to the People of God wherever they were and whatever their social situation. They reacted to God's initiatives in many ways, sometimes rejoicing, at other times rebelling. This journey has been identified by the general editors of *The Renovaré Spiritual Formation Bible* as fifteen expressions of the with-God life (see the following chart). The book you hold in your hand illuminates one dimension, The People of God in Mission. We hope it will help you understand how God has been with his people through the ages and continues to be with us today in our journey toward "the city that has foundations, whose architect and builder is God" (Heb 11:10).

THE PEOPLE OF GOD AND THE WITH-GOD LIFE*

Stage of Formation	Scriptures	God's Action	Human Reaction
I. The People of God in Individual Communion	Genesis 1–11**	Creates, instructs, steward of a good creation, banishes, destroys, restores	Disobey, rebel, sacrifice, murder, repent, obey
II. The People of God Become a Family	Genesis 12–50	Gives promise and establishes Abrahamic covenant, makes a great people	Faith, wrestle with God, persevere
III. The People of God in Exodus	Exodus, Leviticus, Numbers, Deuteronomy	Extends mercy, grace, and deliverance from exile; delivers the Mosaic covenant/law	Obey and disobey, develop a distinctive form of ritual
IV. The People of God in the Promised Land	Joshua, Judges, Ruth, 1 Samuel 1–12	Establishes a theocracy, bequeaths the Promised Land	Inhabit the Promised Land, accept judges as mediators
V. The People of God as a Nation	1 Samuel 13–31 & 2 Samuel, 1 & 2 Kings, 1 & 2 Chronicles, 1 Esdras 1	Permits the monarchy, exalts good kings, uses secular nations for blessing	Embrace the monarchy
VI. The People of God in Travail	Job, Psalms of Lament, Ecclesiastes, Lamentations, Tobit	Permits tribulation, allows suffering to strengthen faith	Complain yet remain faithful
VII. The People of God in Prayer and Worship	Psalms, Psalm 151	Establishes liturgical worship	Praise, prayer
VIII. The People of God in Daily Life	Proverbs, Ecclesiastes, Song of Solomon, Wisdom of Solomon, The Wisdom of Jesus Son of Sirach (Ecclesiasticus)	Gives precepts for living in community	Teachable, learning, treasure beautiful words and artistic expression
IX. The People of God in Rebellion	1 Kings 12–2 Kings 25:10, 2 Chronicles 10–36:19, Isaiah, Jeremiah 1–36, Hosea, Joel, Amos, Jonah, Micah, Nahum, Habakkuk, Zephaniah, Judith, Prayer of Manasseh	Proclaims prophetic judgment and redemption, reveals his rule over all nations, promises Immanuel, uses secular nations to bring judgment	Disbelieve and reject, believe false prophets, a faithful remnant emerges
X. The People of God in Exile	2 Kings 25:11–30, 2 Chronicles 36:20–23, Jeremiah 37–52, Lamentations, Ezekiel, Daniel, Obadiah, Baruch, Letter of Jeremiah, Additions to Daniel	Judges, yet remains faithful to covenant promises	Mourn, survive, long for Jerusalem, stand for God without institutions
XI. The People of God in Restoration	Ezra, Nehemiah, Esther, Daniel, Haggai, Zechariah, Malachi, Additions to Esther, 1 Esdras 2–9, & 2 Esdras, 1, 2, 3, & 4 Maccabees, Tobit, Additions to Daniel	Regathers and redeems, restructures social life	Return, obey, rebuild, worship, pursue Messianic figure, compile Septuagint
XII. The People of God with Immanuel	Matthew, Mark, Luke, John	Sends the Son and acts with the Son	Hear and follow, resist and reject
XIII. The People of God in Mission	Acts	Sends the Holy Spirit and creates the Church	Believe and proclaim, disbelieve and persecute
XIV. The People of God in Community	Romans, 1 & 2 Corinthians, Galatians, Ephesians, Philippians, Colossians, 1 & 2 Thessalonians, 1 & 2 Timothy, Titus, Philemon, Hebrews, James, 1 & 2 Peter, 1, 2, & 3 John, Jude	Builds, nurtures, and mobilizes the Church	Become disciples of Jesus Christ and make disciples to the ends of the earth
XV. The People of God into Eternity	Revelation	Reveals infinite progress toward infinite good	Worship and praise, creativity that magnifies God

* Text taken from *The Renovaré Spiritual Formation Bible.*
** Books are placed into categories by content, not by date of composition or type of literature.

Type of Mediation	Locus of Mediation	Social Context	Central Individual(s)	Key Spiritual Disciplines
Face-to-face	Garden, field, Noah's ark	Individuals	Adam, Eve, Enoch, Noah	Practicing the Presence, confession, sacrifice, obedience/submission
Through the family	Tent, desert, jail	Extended families and nomadic clans	Abraham and Sarah, Isaac, Jacob, Joseph	Pilgrimage, sacrifice, chastity
Through God's terrifying acts and the law	Ark of the covenant, tabernacle	Nomadic tribes	Moses	Submission, silence, simplicity, worship
Through the conquest and learning to act with God	Shiloh, Bethel	An ethnic people with fluid leadership	Joshua, Deborah, Ruth, Samson, Gideon, Samuel	Guidance, radical obedience/submission, secrecy
Through the king, prophets, priests, and sacrifices	Altars, consecrated places, first (Solomonic) Temple	Political nation on the world stage	Saul, David, Hezekiah, Elijah, Elisha	Worship, prayer
Through suffering and the disappointments of life	Ash heap, hard circumstances of life	Individual	Job, Israel as the suffering servant	Fasting, solitude, silence, submission, service, celebration
Through song, prayer, worship	Jerusalem, flowering of individual experience	Nation	David	Prayer, worship, confession, celebration, meditation
Through wisdom	Temple, in the gate, home	Nation triumphant	Solomon	Study, guidance, celebration, meditation
Through the prophets and repression by the Gentiles	High places, Temple desecrated and destroyed	Nation under siege and dispersed	Isaiah, Hosea, Amos	Fasting, repentance, obedience/submission, solitude, silence, the law internalized
Through punishment, being a blessing to their captors	Babylon, anyplace, anytime	Ethnics abroad without a political homeland	Ezekiel, Jeremiah	Detachment, fasting, simplicity, prayer, silence, service
Through repentance, service, synagogue study	Rebuilt Temple, synagogue	Remnant on the international scene, ethnics in the leadership of other nations	Ezra, Cyrus the Persian, Nehemiah, Maccabees, Essenes, John the Baptist	Pilgrimage, confession, worship, study, service
Through the Incarnate Word and the living presence of the kingdom	Temple and synagogue, boats and hillsides, gatherings of disciples	Small groups, disciples, apostles, hostile critics	Jesus Christ Incarnate	Celebration, study, pilgrimage, submission, prayer, sacrifice, obedience, confession
Through the Holy Spirit, persecution, and martyrdom	Temple, synagogue, schools, riversides, public square	Jew, Gentile, house churches, abandonment of social strata	Peter, Paul	Speaking and hearing the word, sacrifice, guidance, generosity/service, fasting, prayer
In one another, through Scripture, teaching, preaching, prophetic utterance, pastoral care, the Holy Spirit, the sacraments	Gathered community	Community redefined by the Body of Christ, decadent Greco-Roman culture	Peter, Paul, John	Prayer, study, accountability/submission, fellowship
Throughout the cosmos	Focused in the New Jerusalem and extending throughout the cosmos	The Trinity and its community	God the Father, Son, and Holy Spirit; apostles, prophets	Living beyond disciplines

LIVING THE MISSION: AN OVERVIEW

✤

There is no better way to get a sense of how the Church came into being than the book of Acts, formally known as the Acts of the Apostles. A continuation of the Gospel of Luke, Acts traces in vivid narrative the period from one of Jesus's last appearances before his disciples to the apostle Paul's house arrest in Rome, a span of approximately thirty-five years. A synopsis of the early years of the Church, Acts is true to its title. It is full of action. And at the center of every action is the Holy Spirit, so much so that some have suggested the book should be titled "The Acts of the Holy Spirit" because of the huge role the Spirit plays in the drama that unfolds on its pages. Studying the way the disciples allowed the Holy Spirit to guide them as they dealt with every challenge and opportunity that came their way is incredibly helpful as we too seek to live the mission we are called to by Jesus.

In this book we focus on what it means to be a part of a fellowship, part of the community of the Church of Jesus Christ. Throughout *Living the Mission* we point to specific insights we can learn from the events Luke records and the stories he tells as the People of God form communities first in Jerusalem and then radiating outward, much like circles emanate from a stone thrown into a lake. The farther the circles go out and the larger the communities become, the more their actions are scrutinized and opposed. In spite of opposition and human hesitation, the Holy Spirit continues to work through the disciples and to reveal that the kingdom of God is available to everyone here and now. Acts is the story of how the followers of Jesus became the Church. It shows us exactly how those of us who are not able to be in Jesus's physical presence can still follow him, how Jesus is still with us in the Holy Spirit, and how we are called to form communities into which we are forever inviting others.

We invite you to join us as we meet and learn from the first members of the Church as they proclaim and live the good news and make disciples of Jesus Christ.

RECEIVING THE COMMISSION

1

KEY SCRIPTURE: Matthew 28:16–20

DEVOTIONAL READING

DALLAS WILLARD, *The Great Omission*

Undiscipled Disciples

For at least several decades the churches of the Western world have not made discipleship a condition of being a Christian. One is not required to be, or to intend to be, a disciple in order to become a Christian, and one may remain a Christian without any signs of progress toward or in discipleship. Contemporary American churches in particular do not require following Christ in his example, spirit, and teachings as a condition of membership—either of entering into or continuing in fellowship of a denomination or local church. . . .

It is helpful for everyone to read the Devotional and Scripture Readings and do the My Life with God Exercise before the meeting. Begin the meeting with silent prayer, then move directly to Reflecting on My Life with God below.

Great Omissions from the Great Commission

A different model was instituted in the "Great Commission" Jesus left for his people. The first goal he set for the early church was to use his all-encompassing power and authority to make disciples without regard to ethnic distinctions—from all "nations" (Matthew 28:19). . . . Having made disciples, these alone were to be baptized into the name of the Father, and of the Son, and of the Holy Spirit. Given this twofold preparation they were then to be taught to treasure and keep "all things whatsoever I have commanded you" (Matthew 28:20). The Christian church of the first centuries resulted from following this plan for church growth—a result hard to improve upon.

But in place of Christ's plan, historical drift has substituted "Make converts (to a particular 'faith and practice') and baptize them into church membership." This causes two great omissions from the Great Commission to stand out. Most important, we start by omitting the making of disciples and enrolling people as Christ's students, when we should let all else wait for that. Then we also omit, of necessity, the step of taking our converts through training that will bring them ever-increasingly to do what Jesus directed.

These two great omissions are connected in practice into one whole. Not having made our converts disciples, it is *impossible* for us to teach them how to live as Christ lived and taught (Luke 14:26). That was not a part of the package, not what they converted *to*. When confronted with the example and teachings of Christ, the response today is less one of rebellion or rejection than one of puzzlement: How do we relate to these? What do they have to do with us? Isn't this bait and switch?

Discipleship Then

When Jesus walked among humankind there was a certain simplicity to being his disciple. Primarily it meant to go with him, in an attitude of observation, study, obedience, and imitation. There were no correspondence courses. One knew what to do and what it would cost. Simon Peter exclaimed: "Look, we have left everything and followed you" (Mark 10:28). Family and occupations were deserted for long periods to go with Jesus as he walked from place to place announcing, showing, and explaining the here-and-now governance or action of God. Disciples had to be with him to learn how to do what he did.... So when Jesus observed that one must forsake the dearest things—family, "all that he hath," and "his own life also" (Luke 14:26, 33)—insofar as that was necessary to accompany him, he stated a simple fact: it was the only possible doorway to discipleship.

Discipleship Now

Though costly, discipleship once had a very clear, straightforward meaning. The mechanics are not the same today. We cannot literally be with him in the same way as his first disciples could. But the priorities and intentions—the heart or inner attitudes—of disciples are forever the same. In the heart of a disciple there is a *desire,* and there is *decision* or settled intent. Having come to some understanding of what it means, and thus having "counted up the costs," the disciple of Christ desires above all else to be like him.... Given this desire, usually produced by the lives and words of those already in the Way, there is still a decision to be made: the decision to devote oneself to becoming like Christ. The disciple is one who, intent upon becoming Christ-like and so dwelling in *his* "faith and practice," systematically and progressively rearranges his affairs to that end. By these decisions and actions, even today, one enrolls in Christ's training, becomes his pupil or disciple. There is no other way....

A mind cluttered by excuses may make a mystery of discipleship, or it may see it as something to be dreaded. But there is no mystery about desiring and intending to be like someone—that is a very common thing. And if we really do intend to be like Christ, that will be obvious to every thoughtful person around us, as well as to ourselves. Of course, attitudes that define the disciple cannot be realized today by leaving family and business to accompany Jesus on his travels about the countryside. But discipleship can be made concrete by actively learning how to love our enemies, bless those who curse us, walk the second mile with an oppressor—in general, living out the gracious inward transformations of faith, hope, and love. Such acts—carried out by the disciplined person with manifest grace, peace, and joy—make discipleship no less tangible and shocking today than were those desertions of long ago. Anyone who will enter into the Way can verify this, and he or she will at the same time prove that discipleship is far from dreadful.[1]

MY LIFE WITH GOD EXERCISE

Dallas Willard perceives one of the faults of today's church to be that we go out and make not disciples but converts—people who accept a certain church's formula for salvation but are not necessarily in the process of training to be more and more like Jesus. Approaching it in a different way, Oswald Chambers writes, "Jesus Christ did not say—Go and save souls (the salvation of souls is the supernatural work of God), but—'Go and teach,' i.e., disciple, 'all nations,' and you cannot make disciples unless you are a disciple yourself."[2] At this point, we may well wonder: What exactly does it mean to be a disciple? According to Willard, we are disciples of whomever we choose to learn from and emulate: "One thing is sure: You are somebody's disciple. You learned how to live from somebody else. There are no exceptions to this rule, for human beings are just the kind of creatures that have to learn and keep learning from others how to live."[3] Willard tells us that being a disciple of Jesus "meant to go with him, in an attitude of observation, study, obedience, and imitation."[4] It also meant that disciples had to make a deliberate decision to devote themselves to becoming like Christ.

In order to better understand the process Jesus's followers went through as they were learning from him, decide to become a disciple or apprentice or student of someone this week. Ask your spouse, parent, or friend to teach you how to make their signature recipe. Or ask a member of your household to show you how to do something that they normally take care of—caring for a child, managing the budget, or doing the laundry. Perhaps you would like to learn a new hobby or skill—knitting, woodworking, using a computer program, or playing golf, all of which require that you ask a teacher or a friend to instruct you over a long period of time. Another way of apprenticing yourself is to study someone at work. You could ask a good friend who is an electrician or photographer or carpenter or teacher if you could observe them for an hour or so. Choose your mentor carefully. You want someone who knows the subject matter well; you can't be an apprentice to someone if you are not willing to submit to their authority. If it is appropriate in the situation, ask lots of questions. Do your best to understand why the person you are watching does things a certain way, and pay attention to your own feelings about being taught.

REFLECTING ON MY LIFE WITH GOD
Allow each member a few moments to answer this question.

How did you serve your apprenticeship? How did it feel to be in the position of student? What insight did it give you into how the disciples apprenticed themselves to Jesus?

> **SCRIPTURE READING:** MATTHEW 28:16–20

After everyone has had a chance to respond to the question, ask a member to read this passage from Scripture.

Now the eleven disciples went to Galilee, to the mountain to which Jesus had directed them. When they saw him, they worshiped him; but some doubted. And Jesus came and said to them, "All authority in heaven and on earth has been given to me. Go therefore and make disciples of all nations, baptizing them in the name of the Father and of the Son and of the Holy Spirit, and teaching them to obey everything that I have commanded you. And remember, I am with you always, to the end of the age."

What gut reaction do you have as you read this Scripture? What statement of Jesus's is most difficult for you to believe or to relate to your own life? Which is the easiest? Why?

>> **GETTING THE PICTURE**

REFLECTION QUESTION
Allow each person a few moments to respond to this question.

After a brief discussion, choose one person to read this section.

During their almost three years with Jesus, these eleven men learned just what it meant to be disciples. They carefully observed Jesus's every action; when they were ready, they tried to do as he did. When Jesus delivered the Sermon on the Mount, they learned the answers to the two great questions everyone asks—Who is really well off? Who is a genuinely good person?—and then tried to apply them to their own lives.[5] They watched as Jesus healed people and confronted evil, and when they went throughout the region on their own, they were able to do exactly the same things (Luke 9:1–6). The disciples learned that prayer, worship, study, and other spiritual practices were deeply ingrained in Jesus's life and were prerequisites to many things they tried to do, such as casting out demons (Mark 9:29). More than once they watched Jesus bless a few pieces of food, then observed the food multiply until thousands were fed. In the innumerable conversations they had with Jesus, he explained the meaning of parables to help them understand that he was ushering in the kingdom of God and that it was present here and now. After watching both John the Baptist and Jesus, they knew how to baptize people with water (John 3:22–24). Jesus's ministry had been full of action, and they had been in the midst of it learning, observing, experimenting, obeying, imitating, studying—becoming disciples. Their hopes and dreams had been extinguished with Jesus's crucifixion, only to be reignited when he rose from the dead.

It is not clear at what point after his resurrection Jesus appears to the eleven disciples as a group to give them the Great Commission cited in our Scripture Reading. Three of the Gospels record that he had already appeared to a group of disciples at least two times while they were still in Jerusalem following the resurrection (see Mark 16:14; Luke 24:13–43; and John 20:19–31). Most likely the next appearance of Jesus to a group was to seven disciples after they had gone home to Galilee (see John 21:1–25). Then, as the above Scripture passage states, the disciples went to the mountain in Galilee to which Jesus directed them. We have no record of any such instruction from Jesus, but we do know that the disciples were accustomed to obeying Jesus, their teacher, and Matthew tells us that they were continuing to do just this by gathering on the mountain in Galilee. Even after his death and resurrection, they are still very much his disciples, ready to see where his latest instructions will take them.

▶▶▶ GOING DEEPER

Even in a passage as short as Matthew 28:16–20, we learn much about discipleship. First, as Dallas Willard and Oswald Chambers made clear, before we can obey the Great Commission, we must first be disciples. If we are not apprenticed to Jesus, doing our very best to become ever more

Have another member read this section.

like him, we can never hope to teach others to do the same. The commission to the disciples was to make disciples of Jesus Christ who would then make disciples of Jesus Christ who would then make disciples of Jesus Christ, ad infinitum. Somewhere in the history of the Church this message got turned into "preach the gospel" only. In his early travels around England, John Wesley preached the gospel and saved many souls. But later in his travels, he writes, "I was more convinced than ever that preaching like an apostle, without joining together those that are awakened and training them up in the ways of God, is only begetting children for the murderer. How much preaching has there been for these twenty years all over Pembrokeshire! But no regular societies, no discipline, no order or connection; and the consequence is that nine out of ten of the once-awakened are now faster asleep than ever."[6] Wesley sought to solve the problem by establishing groups of various sizes—bands, class meetings, and societies—where people trained to be disciples of Jesus Christ.

At its heart, discipleship is obedience. Even after the terrible shock of Jesus's crucifixion and the exhilaration of the resurrection, the disciples still understood that they were to follow the commands of Jesus. Although doubt permeated some of their minds and hearts, they still went to the mountain in Galilee, just as he had directed them. Later they would also gather in Jerusalem, still trusting and obedient in spite of what must have been great confusion and trepidation about the future. The Scripture passage tells us that doubt remained in the minds and hearts of some of the disciples even as they tried to worship Christ. Sometimes the same is true for us. The Holy Spirit has to work on our hearts before our minds are convinced that Jesus Christ is alive and well and here among us to teach us. We can still obey, however, even in the midst of our doubts.

It is also important to recognize that we do not need to have everything in our lives in perfect order to be a disciple of Jesus Christ. Peter, who vowed that he would never leave Jesus and then denied him three times, did not have his life under control. Neither did the disciples who hid out during and after the resurrection. Nor Thomas, who had to have proof that the man standing before him was really Jesus. Nor the two disciples who failed to recognize Jesus as they were traveling home to Emmaus. If we wait until our lives are perfect before becoming disciples of Jesus Christ, none of us ever would. Jesus meets us where we are right now; if we agree to learn from him, he is willing to show us how to live no matter what our starting point.

Finally, as disciples of Jesus Christ, we are not alone. Jesus knew that we must be in someone's presence in order to be their apprentice, and so he promised that he would be with his disciples always. As the disciples soon realized, this meant that he would always be present with them through the Holy Spirit. The Holy Spirit is always there to be our advocate, our comforter, our helper, our teacher. If we are seeking truth, the Holy Spirit will guide us "into all the truth; for he will not speak on his own, but will speak whatever he hears, and he will declare to you the things that are to come" (John 16:13). If we are seeking to make a difference in the world, the Holy Spirit will give us fruit—love, joy, peace, patience, kindness, generosity, faithfulness, gentleness, and self-control—so that our efforts are not in vain (Gal 5:22–23a). If we are looking for new life and peace, we will find it in the Spirit as he dwells in us (Rom 7:6; 8:1–9a). Jesus promised the Advocate, the Holy Spirit, to his disciples at the Last Supper and right before he ascended into heaven, and as we will see in the next chapter, he was true to his promise (see John 16:4b–7 with Acts 1:5).

After reading these descriptions of a disciple, do you consider yourself to be a disciple of Jesus Christ? Why or why not?

REFLECTION QUESTION
Allow each person a few moments to respond.

▶▶▶▶ POINTING TO GOD

Ignatius of Loyola, the sixteenth-century Christian who founded the Jesuits, is well known for the disciples he taught both during his lifetime and in the centuries afterward through the Jesuit order. Ignatius understood that underlying the Great Commission to make disciples was the truth that one had first to be a disciple. Ignatius came to Christ after suffering injuries to both legs in the Battle of Pamplona in 1521. His injuries gave him time to read many great theological works, including books about the lives of Jesus and numerous saints. His studying inspired Ignatius to devote his own life to emulating Jesus and the saints he read about, particularly Francis of Assisi. After regaining his health, he continued his discipleship by spending several months in a cave. During this time of asceticism, he wrote his famous *Spiritual Exercises*—a series of exercises, meditations, and prayers to be practiced under the guidance of a spiritual director. These exercises became a key part of the way Jesuits are trained.

Ignatius broke his leg again and, during this period of recuperation, read and was profoundly influenced by *The Imitation of Christ* by Thomas à Kempis. He decided to expand his theological education by studying

Choose one member to read this section.

at the University of Paris, where he taught fellow students his *Spiritual Exercises*. By the end of his seven years there, he was an ordained priest with a committed group of six followers. In 1534 they formed the Society of Jesus (Jesuits), with a stated mission "to enter upon hospital and missionary work in Jerusalem, or to go without questioning wherever the pope may direct." Ignatius was chosen as the Father General of the new society, with the responsibility of directing his fellow Jesuits in the ways of Christ. From the requests of bishops around the world, he soon saw a great need for schools to educate both clergy and laypeople. As Ignatius sought to meet this need by directing his fellow Jesuits to found colleges and seminaries around Europe, he came to believe that education was the way to most effectively train new disciples. As he wrote in a letter in 1551, "From among those who are now merely students, in time some will depart to play diverse roles—one to preach and carry on the care of souls, another to government of the land and the administration of justice, and others to other callings. Finally, since young boys become grown men, their good education in life and doctrine will be beneficial to many others, with the fruit expanding more widely every day."[7] Today the Jesuit order is still thriving, known for its many institutions of learning around the world. The order continues to emphasize discipleship to Jesus Christ through its spiritual direction program for members of the order and laypeople. Countless people utilize Ignatius's "Thirty Days" retreat format, a combination of spiritual disciplines, solitude, silence, and spiritual direction.

>>>>> **GOING FORWARD**

Have another person read this section.

Think about the people in your life you have observed, studied, and imitated—from your family to influential teachers or writers. There are likely many people that you have unconsciously imitated because you spent so much time with them. Others you deliberately chose to observe and emulate, by watching them or reading their writings or hearing them speak, by spending as much time with them as you could, by trying to act like they might act in certain situations. It is, of course, this latter, deliberate type of discipleship we must apply to become disciples of Jesus.

But all this talk of deliberate decisions and firm commitments can make discipleship sound like an onerous, thankless task. We often focus so much on the costs of discipleship—leaving the life we know behind—that we downplay or forget entirely the benefits of a life apprenticed to

LIVING THE MISSION

Jesus. As Willard writes, "One of the things that has most obstructed the path of discipleship in our Christian culture today is this idea that it will be a terribly difficult thing that will certainly ruin your life.... And here is the whole point of the much misunderstood teachings of Luke 14. There Jesus famously says one must 'hate' all their family members and their own life also, must take their cross, and must forsake all they own, or they 'cannot be my disciple' (Luke 14:26–27, 33). The entire point of this passage is that as long as one thinks anything may really be more valuable than fellowship with Jesus in his kingdom, one cannot learn from him."[8] Once we truly weigh the benefits of living as Jesus's disciple, what else can we do but accept the challenge with joy?

What about the idea of discipleship is daunting or scary to you? What opportunity does it present to you?

REFLECTION QUESTION
Again, allow each member a few moments to answer this question.

This concludes our look at receiving the commission. In the next chapter we will turn our attention to another avenue of living the mission—how we are empowered by the Spirit.

After everyone has had a chance to respond, the leader reads this paragraph.

Allow some time for members to encourage one another to read the Devotional and Scripture Readings and do the exercise in the following chapter before the next meeting. Then invite the members to be silent for a few moments before leading them in reading the Closing Prayer aloud together.

At the end of the Closing Prayer, the leader asks for a volunteer to lead the next meeting.

CLOSING PRAYER

I will extol you, my God and King,
    and bless your name forever and ever.
Every day I will bless you,
    and praise your name forever and ever.
Great is the LORD, and greatly to be praised;
    his greatness is unsearchable.

One generation shall laud your works to another,
    and shall declare your mighty acts.
On the glorious splendor of your majesty,
    and on your wondrous works, I will meditate.
The might of your awesome deeds shall be proclaimed,
    And I will declare your greatness. (PS 145:1–6)

TAKING IT FURTHER

- As was and is the way with Ignatius of Loyola's *Spiritual Exercises,* we can learn a great deal about how to become more Christlike from

ADDITIONAL EXERCISES

a carefully chosen spiritual director. If you do not have a spiritual director, consider seeking out someone to guide you. This does not have to be someone who calls himself or herself a spiritual director; it could simply be someone you know who has progressed along the path of inner transformation to Christlikeness. If you do not know of anyone or feel uncomfortable asking someone you know, try looking for a nearby retreat center where you can try spiritual direction for the duration of a retreat.

- In Going Deeper, we discussed the idea that we do not have to have our lives in perfect order to be disciples of Jesus Christ. Read John 13:36–38; 18:15–18, 25–27; 20:24–29; and Luke 24:13–31, and think about how Peter, Thomas, and the two disciples traveling to Emmaus, despite their weaknesses, were still able to serve God as disciples. How has God used you in spite of your weaknesses?

ADDITIONAL RESOURCES

Divarkar, Parmananda, and Edward J. Malatesta. *Ignatius of Loyola: Spiritual Exercises and Selected Works.* Mahwah, NJ: Paulist, 1991.

Thomas à Kempis. *The Imitation of Christ.* Translated by William C. Creasy. Notre Dame, IN: Ave Maria, 1989.

Willard, Dallas. *The Divine Conspiracy.* San Francisco: HarperSanFrancisco, 1998.

Willard, Dallas. *The Great Omission.* San Francisco: HarperSanFrancisco, 2006.

ADDITIONAL REFLECTION QUESTIONS

Who have you been a disciple of? Who are the most important teachers in your life?

When you became a Christian or were old enough to understand what it meant for you to be a Christian, did you view it as becoming a disciple of Jesus, seeking to become ever more like him? If not, what was your understanding?

Do you agree with Willard's assertion that modern churches create converts rather than disciples? Why or why not? If so, what might be done to help churches create disciples?

BEING EMPOWERED BY THE SPIRIT

2

KEY SCRIPTURE: Acts 1:1–5, 12–14a; 2:1–13

DEVOTIONAL READING

BILLY GRAHAM, *The Holy Spirit*

Without a doubt one of the most awe-inspiring passages in Scripture relates what the angel said to Mary: "The Holy Spirit will come upon you, and the power of the Most High will over-shadow you; and for that reason the holy offspring will be called the Son of God" (Luke 1:35).... The Holy Spirit was also at work among the disciples of Jesus before Pentecost. We know this because Jesus said of them, "He [the Holy Spirit] abides with you" (John 14:17).... Yet the operation of the Spirit among men in Jesus' day differed from His work today. For in John 7:39 we are told by the apostle John concerning the word of Jesus: "But this He [Jesus] spoke of the Spirit, whom those who believed in Him were to receive; for the Spirit was not yet given, because Jesus was not yet glorified."

Exactly what the difference was the Bible does not reveal completely. However, we know that the coming of the Spirit at Pentecost was in a far greater measure than anything they had ever experienced before.... Unquestionably the coming of the Holy Spirit on the day of Pentecost marked a crucial turning point in the history of God's dealings with the human race.... When I began studying about the Holy Spirit shortly after I became a Christian, one of the first questions I asked myself was: Why did the Holy Spirit have to come? I soon found the answer in my Bible study. He came because He had a work to do in the *world*, in the *Church*, and in the individual *Christian*....

What part does the Holy Spirit play in [the life of the Church]? *First,* the Bible beautifully tells us that the Church was brought into being by Him: "For by one Spirit we were all baptized into one body, whether Jews or Greeks, whether slaves or free, and we were all made to drink of one Spirit. For the Body is not one member, but many" (1 Cor. 12:13, 14).

It is helpful for everyone to read the Devotional and Scripture Readings and do the My Life with God Exercise before the meeting. Begin the meeting with silent prayer, then move directly to Reflecting on My Life with God below.

Second, by the Spirit God lives in the Church: "And in him [Christ] you too are being built together to become a dwelling in which God lives by his Spirit" (Eph. 2:22 NIV). . . . *Third,* the Holy Spirit gives gifts to specific people in the Church "for the equipping of the saints for the work of service, to the building up of the body of Christ" (Eph. 4:12). . . .

It appears that God can take a talent and transform it by the power of the Holy Spirit and use it as a spiritual gift. In fact the difference between a spiritual gift and a natural talent is frequently a cause for speculation by many people. I am not sure we can always draw a sharp line between spiritual gifts and natural abilities—both of which, remember, come ultimately from God. Nor do I believe it is always necessary to make a sharp distinction. On most occasions, however, in the context we are discussing, the gifts I have in mind are supernatural ones the Spirit gives a person for the good of the Church.[1]

MY LIFE WITH GOD EXERCISE

Billy Graham writes about the coming of the Spirit experienced by those gathered in Jerusalem at Pentecost and how the Holy Spirit continues to work today for the sake of the Church. To get more of an idea of the many ways the Holy Spirit worked in biblical times and continues to work among us today, read the following small sample of the many Scripture passages about the Spirit: Matthew 1:18–20; Mark 1:4–13; Luke 1:39–45; 11:9–13; 12:11–12; John 14:26; Romans 5:5; 7:6; 8:26–27; 1 Corinthians 2:13; 12:4–11; and Galatians 5:16–25. While you're reading, keep these questions in mind:

- What are some of the actions of the Spirit described in these passages?
- How do these fit with your understanding of the Holy Spirit and how it works in the Church, in your own life?
- What has been your own personal experience of the Holy Spirit?
- Have you experienced the Holy Spirit in any of the ways described here? For example, did you have a sense of being filled with the Spirit when you became a Christian or were baptized? Did the Holy Spirit perhaps provide you with words during a difficult time or help you discern a particularly thorny theological topic or personal crisis? Have you been blessed with certain gifts or fruit of the Spirit?

- Overall, do you feel that you experience the Spirit often, or are you not sure if or how the Holy Spirit is working in your life?

If you like, study further by using a concordance to help you find more passages about the Spirit. Ask God to help you understand and recognize the workings of the Holy Spirit in your own life, in the Church, and in the world today.

What understanding did you gain about the Holy Spirit? What is one way you feel you have experienced the Holy Spirit in your life?

REFLECTING ON MY LIFE WITH GOD
Allow each member a few moments to answer this question.

➤ SCRIPTURE READING: ACTS 1:1–5, 12–14A; 2:1–13

In the first book, Theophilus, I wrote about all that Jesus did and taught from the beginning until the day when he was taken up to heaven, after giving instructions through the Holy Spirit to the apostles whom he had chosen. After his suffering he presented himself alive to them by many convincing proofs, appearing to them during forty days and speaking about the kingdom of God. While staying [or eating] with them, he ordered them not to leave Jerusalem, but to wait there for the promise of the Father. "This," he said, "is what you have heard from me; for John baptized with water, but you will be baptized with the Holy Spirit not many days from now." . . .

Then [the apostles] returned to Jerusalem from the mount called Olivet, which is near Jerusalem, a sabbath day's journey away. When they had entered the city, they went to the room upstairs where they were staying, Peter and John, and James, and Andrew, Philip and Thomas, Bartholomew and Matthew, James son of Alphaeus, and Simon the Zealot, and Judas son of James. All these were constantly devoting themselves to prayer. . . .

When the day of Pentecost had come . . . suddenly from heaven there came a sound like the rush of a violent wind, and it filled the entire house where they were sitting. Divided tongues, as of fire, appeared among them, and a tongue rested on each of them. All of them were filled with the Holy Spirit and began to speak in other languages, as the Spirit gave them ability.

Now there were devout Jews from every nation under heaven living in Jerusalem. And at this sound the crowd gathered and was bewildered, because each one heard them speaking in the native language of each. Amazed and astonished, they asked, "Are not all these who are speaking

✍ After everyone has had a chance to respond to the question, ask a member to read this passage from Scripture.

Galileans? And how is it that we hear, each of us, in our own native language? Parthians, Medes, Elamites, and residents of Mesopotamia, Judea and Cappadocia, Pontus and Asia, Phrygia and Pamphylia, Egypt and the parts of Libya belonging to Cyrene, and visitors from Rome, both Jews and proselytes, Cretans and Arabs—in our own languages we hear them speaking about God's deeds of power." All were amazed and perplexed, saying to one another, "What does this mean?" But others sneered and said, "They are filled with new wine."

What insight does this passage give us about the Holy Spirit?

REFLECTION QUESTION
Allow each person a few moments to respond to this question.

▶▶ GETTING THE PICTURE

⌇ After a brief discussion, choose one person to read this section.

All Jewish males who lived within twenty miles of Jerusalem were legally bound to attend three festivals: Pentecost, Passover, and the Feast of Tabernacles. Because Pentecost was celebrated fifty days after Passover and Jesus rose from the dead on the first day after Passover, we know that at this point it had been almost fifty days since his resurrection.

The festival of Pentecost commemorated Moses receiving the law on Mount Sinai. After the events in the Scripture Reading, however, Pentecost took on a whole new meaning for Jesus's followers. The events at Pentecost showed how they were to move forward after Jesus's time as a human being. Pentecost introduced the People of God to living and proclaiming the kingdom of God in the power of the Holy Spirit. On this day the Church was born from the Holy Spirit, whose presence was accompanied by supernatural signs and powerful witness.

As we discussed in the last chapter, the eleven remaining disciples from Jesus's inner circle went to Galilee after the resurrection; there Jesus appeared to seven of them as they were fishing, then to all eleven on a mountain, where they received what we call the Great Commission (Matt 28:18–20). They then returned to Jerusalem, where Jesus again appeared, giving further instructions about what they were to do and how they would do it: "That repentance and forgiveness of sins is to be proclaimed in [Jesus's] name to all nations, beginning from Jerusalem. You are witnesses of these things. And see, I am sending upon you what my Father promised; so stay here in the city until you have been clothed with power from on high" (Luke 24:47–49; see also Acts 1:7–8). This power from on high, this new expression of the Holy Spirit, was not unexpected; the Holy Spirit had been active long before Pentecost.

The Old Testament shows us that the Holy Spirit was present from the beginning, at Creation, and worked throughout the time before Jesus lived by coming upon certain people for particular tasks or blessings.[2] Further, prophets such as Joel had predicted a day when a new age of the Spirit would be ushered in: "In those days, I will pour out my spirit" (Joel 2:29b; see also Acts 2:18b). John the Baptist preached that whereas he baptized only with water, Jesus would be baptizing with the Holy Spirit and fire (Matt 3:11).

Meanwhile, the apostles, mindful of these expectations but certainly not knowing exactly what was ahead, returned to the room where they were staying in Jerusalem after observing Jesus ascend into heaven from Mount Olivet. It was in this room that the eleven, along with other disciples, including Mary, Jesus's mother, and his brothers, devoted themselves to prayer. And it was in this upstairs room that Peter emerged as the leader among the apostles, and Matthias was chosen to replace Judas Iscariot.

At this point the Spirit comes upon the twelve apostles and the others in the room with three distinct, supernatural signs—a sound like wind, tongues as of fire that rested on each of them, and an outpouring of speech, as they speak and are heard in many different languages. The Spirit is here.

▶▶▶ GOING DEEPER

The implications for Christians today of the Spirit coming upon Jesus's followers at Pentecost are numerous. Perhaps most importantly, we now know that the Spirit is available to all of us and that all who trust in Jesus are filled with the Spirit—not just those chosen for special service, as was the case in the Old Testament. In this passage we see that God's Spirit came upon *everyone* who was open to God. Luke makes it clear that there were people of many backgrounds in the room—from the apostles whom Jesus had personally trained to Jesus's mother and brothers. In his Gospel Luke wrote that many women traveled with Jesus, some of whom financed his travels (Luke 8:1–3), and that at least seventy disciples received personal training (Luke 10:1–20). We do not know if all of them were in the room as it filled with the Holy Spirit, but we do know that *all* of the people in that room were believers, and *all* were filled with the Holy Spirit regardless of education or religious position or business success. The fact that the Spirit is available to everyone is made more evident later, when Peter goes to the house of Cornelius, a Gentile,

Have another member read this section.

to tell the good news. As he begins to speak, Peter says, "'I truly understand that God shows no partiality. . . .' While Peter was still speaking, the Holy Spirit fell upon all who heard the word" (Acts 10:34b, 44).

The Holy Spirit is how Jesus is with us, his people, his Church. The Holy Spirit guides us as we grow in spiritual maturity; we also receive gifts of the Spirit similar to those received by the followers at Pentecost, gifts such as preaching, teaching, and discernment, gifts designed to build up the Church. The gift of speaking in other languages on the day of Pentecost empowered Jesus's followers to tell the good news of his birth, life, death, and resurrection. As John Stott writes, "It was the fulfillment not only of the general Old Testament expectation of the Spirit's coming, but also of those special promises of Jesus in the Upper Room which were addressed primarily to the apostles and whose fulfillment was intended to equip them for their particular apostolic work as inspired and authoritative teachers."[3] Today the Spirit similarly equips us "for the work of ministry, for building up the body of Christ" (Eph 4:12).

The fruit and gifts of the Spirit are supernatural and thus given to us, not earned, but we can work to create the conditions within our souls that make us fertile ground. The followers of Jesus prepared themselves with prayer as they were waiting to be "clothed with power from on high." We, too, can open ourselves to the work of the Spirit through similar preparation.

One of the most important manifestations of the coming of the Spirit, which receives much attention in Luke's account, is the supernatural way believers spoke in various languages so that pilgrims in Jerusalem could hear the message of God in their own language. While we know that the Spirit helps us with individual matters of guidance and discernment, another important way the Spirit equips us for mission is by helping us to communicate with and relate to those around us. The Spirit helps us to share the gospel in intelligible ways and also helps those to whom we are speaking understand us and hear our message.

When has the Spirit helped you to communicate or to understand?

▶▶▶▶ POINTING TO GOD

One of the most shocking things about the Spirit entering into Jesus's followers on that long-ago Pentecost was that it entered into all of them, not just the twelve apostles. This inclusiveness of the work of the Spirit was also evident in the modern-day Pentecost of William Seymour and the Azusa Street Revival in the early twentieth century. Seymour was the son of slaves. As a young man, he was influenced by Charles Parham's teachings about the Holy Spirit, namely that God always gives intelligible languages to those trying to evangelize. Seymour was invited to serve as preacher at the Second Baptist Church in Los Angeles, where he taught that speaking in tongues (glossolalia) was evidence of baptism in the Holy Spirit. His teachings were controversial, and they were initially rejected by the church's head pastor, but Seymour and a group of church members met at the home of one member and began to experience glossolalia. The group eventually rented a large ramshackle building of their own on Azusa Street. There overflowing crowds gathered as many were overcome by the power of the Spirit. The *Los Angeles Daily Times* reported that a strange new "sect of fanatics" had formed, with people "breathing strange utterances and mouthing a creed which it would seem no sane mortal could understand. . . . Colored people and a sprinkling of whites compose the congregation, and night is made hideous in the neighborhood by the howlings of the worshippers who spend hours swaying forth and back in a nerve-racking attitude of prayer and supplication."[4]

Excitement about the revival spread quickly, despite its detractors, as participants traveled and wrote about their experiences, and people came from all over the world to see and experience the outpouring of the Spirit, including many missionaries who hoped to receive the gift of languages to aid in their mission work. The revival at the building on Azusa Street lasted for three years, from 1906 to 1909, and formed the roots of today's Pentecostal and Charismatic movements. It was remarkable not only for its radical demonstration of the power of the Spirit but also for its inclusivity. Although Jim Crow laws had forced Seymour to sit in the hall and listen to Parham's teachings through an open door, his church at Azusa Street was open to all. African-Americans, whites, and Latinos worshiped together, a practice remarkable for the time. The egalitarian focus of the church extended past racial lines, too. All attendees at Azusa were potential contributors to the service, exemplified by the positioning of benches in the building all on one level, with no raised platform at the front for a pulpit.[5] But not all were fans of the church's racially inclusive style. When Seymour's early mentor, Charles Parham, visited the church, he was horrified by the mixing of the races in worship. However, participants like Frank Bartleman treasured the unity brought by the enthusiastic worship. "The color line was washed away in the blood [of Jesus Christ]," he said.[6]

►►►► GOING FORWARD

✍ Have another person read this section.

The examples of Pentecost and the Azusa Street Revival are exciting stories of the power of the Spirit, but they are not meant to be normative. If we do not hear sounds like a wind, see tongues like flames, or speak in other languages, this in no way means that we are not filled with the Holy Spirit. The rest of the New Testament makes it clear that all those who trust in Jesus become filled with the Holy Spirit.

But what exactly does it mean to be empowered by the Holy Spirit? We can be sure that each of us will experience the Holy Spirit differently, according to our own gifts and even our own personalities. But there are some common characteristics of being Spirit-filled. We know we are filled with the Spirit when we display the fruit of the Spirit: love, joy, peace, patience, kindness, generosity, faithfulness, gentleness, and self-control (Gal 5:22–23a). The apostle Paul tells us in Ephesians, "[Be] filled with the Spirit. Speak to one another with psalms, hymns and spiritual songs. Sing and make music in your heart to the Lord, always giving thanks to God the Father for everything in the name of our Lord Jesus Christ" (18b–20, NIV). From these words we can see that being filled with the Spirit means fellowship. It means worship. It means thanksgiving, thanking God for *everything*. As John R. W. Stott wrote, "Let us constantly seek to be filled with the Spirit, to be led by the Spirit, to walk with the Spirit.... We all need to hear and obey the gracious invitation of Jesus: 'If any one thirst, let him come to me and drink.' We must learn to come to Jesus and to keep drinking. Only so, in the wise and balanced language of the Book of Common Prayer, shall we 'daily increase in the Holy Spirit more and more, until we come unto God's everlasting kingdom.'"[7]

REFLECTION QUESTION
Again, allow each member a few moments to answer this question.

What are you doing to remain continuously in touch with the Spirit?

✍ After everyone has had a chance to respond, the leader reads this paragraph.

This concludes our look at being empowered by the Spirit. In the next chapter we will turn our attention to another avenue of living the mission—how the early Church became a community.

CLOSING PRAYER

I will extol you, my God and King,
  and bless your name forever and ever.
Every day I will bless you,
  and praise your name forever and ever.
Great is the LORD, and greatly to be praised;
  his greatness is unsearchable.

One generation shall laud your works to another,
  and shall declare your mighty acts.
On the glorious splendor of your majesty,
  and on your wondrous works, I will meditate.
The might of your awesome deeds shall be proclaimed,
  And I will declare your greatness. (PS 145:1–6)

↪ Allow some time for members to encourage one another to read the Devotional and Scripture Readings and do the exercise in the following chapter before the next meeting. Then invite the members to be silent for a few moments before leading them in reading the Closing Prayer aloud together.

↪ At the end of the Closing Prayer, the leader asks for a volunteer to lead the next meeting.

TAKING IT FURTHER

ADDITIONAL EXERCISES

- One of the many ways the Holy Spirit works today is the bestowing of spiritual gifts. Read or reread Romans 12:6–8; 1 Corinthians 12:4–11, 27–28; and Ephesians 4:11–13, and jot down the various spiritual gifts you see listed there. Do you feel you have been given any of these gifts? A good way to determine your own spiritual gifts is to ask friends and fellow church members; often those around us can see us more clearly than we see ourselves. If you are still having trouble discerning your own spiritual gifts, seek out an inventory or test to help you determine in what direction your spiritual strengths lie. There are many tests of this type available on the Internet, or you might want to look in your church library for a denominational test.

- Consider attending a church that may have a different attitude toward the Holy Spirit than your own. For example, you might try to attend a Pentecostal or Charismatic service, if that is not your tradition. If it is, you could attend a service at a church outside the Pentecostal tradition.

ADDITIONAL RESOURCES

Foster, Richard J. *Streams of Living Water*. San Francisco: HarperSanFrancisco, 1998.

Graham, Billy. *The Holy Spirit,* Waco, TX: Word, 1978.

Hollenweger, Walter J. *Pentecostalism: Origins and Developments Worldwide*. Peabody, MA: Hendrickson, 1997.

McGee, Gary B. "William Seymour and the Azusa Street Revival." *Enrichment Journal.* Available at http://www.ag.org/ enrichmentjournal/199904/026_azusa.cfm.

Stott, John R. W. *Baptism and Fullness: The Work of the Holy Spirit Today.* Downers Grove, IL: InterVarsity, 1975.

ADDITIONAL REFLECTION QUESTIONS

How do you most clearly see the Holy Spirit working in your life?

What are some spiritual gifts you would add to the lists in the New Testament (Rom 12:6–8; 1 Cor 12:4–11, 27–28; and Eph 4:11)?

It is often said that the Holy Spirit is either overemphasized or ignored in most churches today. Do you agree? Which of these, if either, do you think applies to your own church tradition? What might be done to create more balance?

FORMING A COMMUNITY

3

KEY SCRIPTURE: Acts 2:42–47; 4:32–37

DEVOTIONAL READING

JEAN VANIER, *Community and Growth*

I love that passage from the Bible: 'And I will say ... "You are my people"; and he shall say "Thou art my God"' (Hosea 2:23).

I shall always remember one of Martin Luther King's disciples, saying to a gathering of many thousands of blacks in Chicago, in the early seventies: 'My people are humiliated.' Mother Teresa of Calcutta says, 'My people are hungry.'

'My people' are my community, which is both the small community, those who live together, and the larger community which surrounds it and for which it is there. 'My people' are those who are written in my flesh as I am in theirs. Whether we are near each other or far away, my brothers and sisters remain written within me. I carry them, and they, me; we recognise each other again when we meet. To call them 'my people' doesn't mean that I feel superior to them, or that I am their shepherd or that I look after them. I mean that they are mine as I am theirs. There is a solidarity between us. What touches them, touches me. And when I say 'my people,' I don't imply that there are others I reject. My people is my community, made up of those who know me and carry me. They are a springboard towards all humanity. I cannot be a universal brother or sister unless I first love my people. ...

People come together because they are of the same flesh and blood, or of the same village and tribe; some wanting security and comfort come together because they are alike and have the same vision of themselves and of the world; some come together because they want to grow in universal love and compassion. It is these latter who create true community.

The difference between community and a group of friends is that in a community we verbalise our mutual belonging and bonding. We announce the goals and the spirit that unites us. We recognise together

⊲ It is helpful for everyone to read the Devotional and Scripture Readings and do the My Life with God Exercise before the meeting. Begin the meeting with silent prayer, then move directly to Reflecting on My Life with God below.

that we are responsible for one another. We recognise also that this bonding comes from God; it is a gift from God. It is he who has chosen us and called us together in a covenant of love and mutual caring. But, of course, a group of friends can become a community, when its sense of belonging grows and opens to others, and when little by little people begin to feel truly responsible for each other.[1]

MY LIFE WITH GOD EXERCISE

The term *community* can mean many things: the church fellowship where we donate our money, time, and talent; the cooperative house we live in; the town where we reside; the twelve-step program we attend; the professional organization we belong to; and so on. For Jean Vanier, the founder of the international l'Arche communities (see Pointing to God), community consists of the brothers and sisters with whom he shares a mutual sense of belonging and responsibility, those whom he calls "my people."

Who are your people? How does community manifest itself in your life? Take a few minutes to create a visual representation of at least some of the communities in which you are involved. One way to do this is to draw something in the middle of your paper that represents you, then use circles that partially encompass your symbol to represent the communities of which you are a part, starting with the smaller circle of your immediate family and then moving on to the larger circles of your work, school, or town. Some circles will be encompassed within others—for example, your immediate family may be contained within a circle of your larger extended family, or certain activities or small groups might be contained within your larger group, school, church, or work circle. Other circles may represent communities you lived in or belonged to in the past. Take as much time with this as you would like, making sure to consider all the different communities in which you take part. You might like to work in pencil, at least at first, as you think about new communities to include and how the communities relate to one another.

Once you have completed your diagram, consider the different communities listed there. Which of these would you identify as "my people," to use Vanier's term? Choose the one that you feel most closely represents "your people," preferably a community in which you are more intimately involved—for example, your immediate family or your small group or a close group of friends, rather than larger communities such as your town, state, or country. Think about the way your example works as a community, what you share, the benefits each member receives, what each member gives. Do you each have a sense of responsibility for one another? If so, how does that manifest itself? What is your role in the community?

As you are reflecting, read and study 1 Corinthians 13, which is Paul's answer to those in the church at Corinth who were disrupting their community's life through partisanship, arrogance, and inconsideration of each other's welfare. What insights does this passage give you about the nature of community? Keeping the passage in mind, think about a way in which you can promote this kind of shared love within your chosen community. It may be as simple as resolving to show patience and kindness to a person who always interrupts in your small group or offering to take on an additional responsibility, such as hosting a meal for your community or a part of it. Or perhaps you will feel called to a larger gesture, such as making a commitment to help out another member financially or personally or taking on a leadership role.

What did you discover about Christian community, both in general and in your life, during your reflections and your study of 1 Corinthians 13? What did you do to promote a sense of shared love and responsibility within your community?

REFLECTING ON MY LIFE WITH GOD
Allow each member a few moments to answer this question.

▶ SCRIPTURE READING: ACTS 2:42–47; 4:32–37

They devoted themselves to the apostles' teaching and fellowship, to the breaking of bread and the prayers.

After everyone has had a chance to respond to the question, ask a member to read this passage from Scripture.

Awe came upon everyone, because many wonders and signs were being done by the apostles. All who believed were together and had all things in common; they would sell their possessions and goods and distribute the proceeds to all, as any had need. Day by day, as they spent much time together in the temple, they broke bread at home and ate their food with glad and generous hearts, praising God and having the goodwill of all the people. And day by day the Lord added to their number those who were being saved....

Now the whole group of those who believed were of one heart and soul, and no one claimed private ownership of any possessions, but everything they owned was held in common. With great power the apostles gave their testimony to the resurrection of the Lord Jesus, and grace was upon them all. There was not a needy person among them, for as many as owned lands or houses sold them and brought the proceeds of what was sold. They laid it at the apostles' feet, and it was distributed to each as any had need. There was a Levite, a native of Cyprus, Joseph, to whom the apostles gave the name Barnabas (which means "son of encouragement"). He sold a field that belonged to him, then brought the money, and laid it at the apostles' feet.

REFLECTION QUESTION
Allow each person a few moments to respond to this question.

What reaction do you have to the early Christian community's practice of holding all possessions in common and distributing according to need the proceeds of the sale of private property? Is this kind of practice applicable to contemporary society? Why or why not?

▶▶ GETTING THE PICTURE

✒ After a brief discussion, choose one person to read this section.

When teaching about the relationship of people to each other, Jesus never used the word *community* or *congregation*. However, his Sermon on the Mount and many other teachings *assume* the existence of a community. For example: "So when you are offering your gift at the altar, if you remember that your brother or sister has something against you, leave your gift there before the altar and go; first be reconciled to your brother or sister, and then come and offer your gift" (Matt 5:23–24); "If any of you put a stumbling block before one of these little ones who believe in me, it would be better for you if a great millstone were hung around your neck and you were thrown into the sea" (Mark 9:42); "But I say to you that listen, Love your enemies, do good to those who hate you, bless those who curse you, pray for those who abuse you" (Luke 6:27–28). The idea of community is implicit throughout. All Israelites were quite aware they belonged to the same community because they were bound together by a common ancestor, Abraham, and a common faith, Judaism. It was in their genes and in their Scriptures.

This strong sense of community inherited from Judaism bound the disciples together as they followed Jesus's instructions and waited to be "baptized with the Holy Spirit" (Acts 1:5). But there was something else happening that helped form them into a community markedly different from their Jewish heritage. Many of them had given up their occupations and their assets to wander around the countryside with Jesus for three years. Leaving homes and families, they had suffered, gone hungry, and been afraid together. They knew each other's strengths and weaknesses and hurts: John's steadfastness, Peter's impulsiveness, Thomas's doubt, Mary's grief. On the day of Pentecost they were empowered by the Holy Spirit, spoke in foreign languages, and baptized three thousand people into their fellowship. All these events led the disciples to realize that they were all in the same boat, prepared to sink or swim together as they faced an unknown future. But they now had the Holy Spirit, which, along with their devotion "to the apostles' teaching and fellowship, to the breaking of bread and the prayers," was the glue that held them together and led to their oneness of heart.

The disciples' reaction to what was happening in their midst is a direct outworking of Jesus's teaching. His emphasis on caring for one another and his prayer that the disciples "may all be one" as he and the Father were one were coming to fruition (John 17:21). This oneness, this transparency, this vulnerability, this openness to each other and to the workings of the Holy Spirit have an immediate and enduring impact on the life of the community. A reverential awe permeates it as they see the Holy Spirit work miracles and bring more people into their fellowship in spite of opposition from the religious leaders (Acts 3–4:31). They begin to look out for the needs of those who have limited resources. Selfishness and hardheartedness give way to generosity and tenderness. And the whole group submits to the authority of the twelve apostles as they preach the resurrection of Jesus Christ and distribute "to each as any had need." But this is no ordinary community based on humanistic ethics or laws. This community is built on belief in the resurrected Jesus Christ and validated by the presence of the Holy Spirit in its midst: "When they had prayed, the place in which they were gathered together was shaken; and they were all filled with the Holy Spirit and spoke the word of God with boldness" (4:31).

▶▶▶ GOING DEEPER

Villages and towns in Jesus's time shared their sources of water (wells and springs) and sanitary facilities (communal baths and latrines), and many times neighbors traveled together in groups to avoid being attacked by bandits and robbers (see Luke 2:41–51 with 10:29–37). Small homes were built close together, and neighbors and servants alike interacted at outdoor ovens. Unfortunately, our culture today is designed to keep us from interacting. Our water, sanitary facilities, and cooking appliances are all inside our comparatively large homes, and we travel down highways isolated in our own automobiles. When we travel with a group of people in public transportation such as buses, trains, and airplanes, we do not know our fellow travelers, and generally make no effort to become acquainted with them. All of these factors mitigate against a sense of community in our culture. This attitude has crossed over to our churches as well. We often

Have another member read this section.

worship in a bubble, lost in our own thoughts, nodding friendly hellos and goodbyes to our fellow church members but not really forming and sustaining a strongly knit family and community as Jesus intended—the kind of community exemplified in passages such as our Scripture Reading.

So what can we learn from Luke's description of the young Christian community that can help us build the sense of community Jesus intended for his followers? Christianity is a faith formed and nurtured in community, so it is of the utmost importance to our own spiritual nourishment that we belong to a community, whether this takes the form of a church, a small group within a church, or even a shared living situation with other Christians. The Holy Spirit empowered a community to proclaim the gospel to people from numerous and varied language groups on the day of Pentecost. It was in community that the apostles accomplished many wonders and signs. Even though Luke records some solitary examples of people being empowered by the Holy Spirit outside the context of a community (for instance, Philip's encounter with the Ethiopian eunuch), by and large the Spirit works through the community and the individuals in that community to bring people into the kingdom of God. So it is today. We must belong to a community of fellow travelers in order to be spiritually nourished to the fullest extent possible. And this is not just for our own spiritual benefit. It is arranged this way so we can be God's representatives *in* the world to communicate the gospel *to* the world.

What should this community look like? A Christian community has at its center "teaching and fellowship, ... the breaking of bread and the prayers." The first element, teaching, consists of reinforcing for present disciples and instructing new disciples about the ways of Jesus so that we can follow them (Matt 28:20). The second element, fellowship, involves opening our lives to each other, being together in good times and bad, in leisure and in study. It also means being transparent and open with each other, sharing our dreams and our struggles so that we can receive and give encouragement, support, and help. The third element, breaking of bread, means sharing the Lord's Supper together, but it also means eating regular meals together and sharing in the important events in one another's lives. The fourth element, prayer, means praying together as a community for wisdom and discernment, for boldness to tell the world about Jesus Christ, for guidance and direction in our work in the world, that the sick and infirm may get well, that political and religious leaders may make wise decisions, that those who don't know Christ and those who are hard-hearted may open their hearts to the love of Christ, and much more. These four elements are at the center of any Christian community.

In order to truly engage in the teaching, fellowship, breaking of bread, and prayer that are the hallmarks of Christian community, we must be willing to invest ourselves in relationships with other people, just as Jesus invested himself in relationships with his disciples. After being empowered by the Holy Spirit, the early church community saw three thousand people come into its fellowship on the day of Pentecost. The disciples and apostles then started devoting their lives to meeting the spiritual and physical needs of new believers in the community. They had learned from Jesus that at the heart of serving God is the serving of others. There is really no better way to learn and grow in Christlikeness.

Today, in a culture that emphasizes self-reliance, being in fellowship with others and coming to depend on them may initially seem scary. It is much easier to trust only ourselves, to hold back from genuine interaction with others, afraid to need others and afraid to lay our souls bare for fear that we will be rejected or taken advantage of. It is a hard thing to let ourselves become vulnerable. Yet this is just what God asks of us: to be vulnerable not only to him in our prayer life but also to those in our community. To get over our fears, to open our hearts and to trust God to overcome whatever personality conflicts and disagreements and difficulties arise. Tough words. But words that bring us back to the foundational statement of *The Renovaré Spiritual Formation Bible*: "The aim of God in history is the creation of an all-inclusive community of loving persons with God himself at the very center of this community as its prime Sustainer and most glorious inhabitant."[2] Until that time comes, the Holy Spirit is at the center of our community, sustaining and teaching and correcting and discipling us through our fellow members.[3]

In your Christian faith, what importance do you place on community in comparison to disciplines like prayer and Bible study?

REFLECTION QUESTION
Allow each person a few moments to respond.

▶▶▶▶ POINTING TO GOD

Even in modern times, many communities try to follow the practices of the early Church, for example, l'Arche communities in Toronto, Paris, and around the world. Jean Vanier, the founder of l'Arche, was born in Canada, in 1928, the son of Georges P. Vanier, the former governor general of Canada. Vanier received a doctorate in philosophy from the Institut Catholique in Paris. In 1964, a Dominican priest, Father Thomas Philippe, showed Vanier some of the problems faced by the thousands of

✐ Choose one member to read this section.

Forming a Community

31

people institutionalized with developmental disabilities. Vanier was so moved by their plight that he invited two disabled men, Raphaël Simi and Philippe Seux, to leave their institutions and live with him in a home in Trosly-Breuil, France. They called this home l'Arche, after Noah's ark.

From this original community, 103 more communities have been formed around the world.[4] L'Arche communities are faith-based service organizations that use a community model of living rather than the medical model favored by many institutions and hospitals. At l'Arche homes and day programs, people with disabilities and those who assist them share equal responsibility and decision-making for their homes and communities.[5] Each member of the community contributes as he or she is able, through employment, leadership of daytime activities, and financial support. Mutuality in relationships is a central tenet of life at l'Arche, and one of Vanier's founding principles was that living together in community enables members to learn from one another.

Catholic priest and author Henri Nouwen, who lived in l'Arche communities from 1985 until his death in 1996, wrote about how moved he was by the simplicity, directness, and intimacy of the prayers of the handicapped people he met during his first year at l'Arche in France. As he gained a new appreciation for the importance of patience, human dignity, and ministering to the body as well as to the spirit, he eventually came to believe that living in this type of community was God's will for his life. As he wrote in his journal that first year, "The glory of God stands in contrast to the glory of people. People seek glory by moving upward. God reveals his glory by moving downward. If we truly want to see the glory of God, we must move downward with Jesus. This is the deepest reason for living in solidarity with poor, oppressed, and handicapped people. They are the ones through whom God's glory can manifest itself to us. They show us the way to God, the way to salvation. This is what L'Arche is beginning to teach me."[6]

▶▶▶▶▶ GOING FORWARD

🖎 Have another person read this section.

The sense of community the disciples knew from being Israelites, the tight-knit fellowship they shared when they followed Jesus and learned from him—these beginnings served as preparation for the community created in the early Church. We see no stories in the New Testament of followers of Jesus who went it alone, at least not by choice. All of them participated in a shared life. Even later, in Acts and the Epistles, when

Paul is on his various missionary journeys, he often mentions in his letters how he longs to be back in the communities he has planted (Phil 1:8; 1 Thess 3:6). Community is an essential component of our spiritual growth. Eugene Peterson writes, "There can be no maturity in the spiritual life, no obedience in following Jesus, no wholeness in the Christian life apart from an immersion and embrace of community."[7]

Our participation in community is not only for our own spiritual benefit but for the larger community around us. When we are able to love as Paul describes in 1 Corinthians 13, when we are able to share in a sense of mutual responsibility, belonging, and caring, as Vanier describes in the Devotional Reading, then we are able not only to provide an undeniably powerful witness to the way of Christ, but also to accomplish so much more of God's kingdom work in the world around us. So we share our problems and our triumphs with our friends and our small group; we reach out to fellow church members, colleagues, and neighbors by sharing social time with them and offering them help and support when they are struggling; we constantly seek to make our community ever wider and more diverse by opening it to people of all stripes. We seek to develop a sense of mutual belonging and responsibility to one another, all while recognizing that Jesus is at the center of everything we do. We realize that the abundant life is life together.

The Scripture Reading describes the early church community as being "of one heart and soul." What does this description mean to you? Is it true of your church? If not, what would such a community look like?

REFLECTION QUESTION
Again, allow each member a few moments to answer this question.

This concludes our look at forming a community. In the next chapter we will turn our attention to another avenue of living the mission—preaching the good news.

✍ After everyone has had a chance to respond, the leader reads this paragraph.

✍ **Allow some time for members to encourage one another to read the Devotional and Scripture Readings and do the exercise in the following chapter before the next meeting.** Then invite the members to be silent for a few moments before leading them in reading the Closing Prayer aloud together.

CLOSING PRAYER

I will extol you, my God and King,
    and bless your name forever and ever.
Every day I will bless you,
    and praise your name forever and ever.
Great is the LORD, and greatly to be praised;
    his greatness is unsearchable.

One generation shall laud your works to another,
    and shall declare your mighty acts.

At the end of the Closing Prayer, the leader asks for a volunteer to lead the next meeting.

On the glorious splendor of your majesty,
and on your wondrous works, I will meditate.
The might of your awesome deeds shall be proclaimed,
And I will declare your greatness. (PS 145:1–6)

TAKING IT FURTHER

ADDITIONAL EXERCISES

- Small groups, what John Wesley referred to as "bands," are a tried-and-true way for Christians to experience community and grow spiritually. If your church has a small-group ministry that you are not participating in, consider joining one of the groups. If your faith community has no such ministry, consider meeting with your pastor to talk about how to pursue such a ministry. If you are already in a small group, consider getting together to brainstorm ways that you can increase the sense of community among your members.

- First Corinthians 13 is a much-loved and often-quoted passage of the Bible. If you do not already know it by heart, try to memorize this short chapter. Here are a few different methods you could use to assist in the process of memorization. 1) Write out each verse over and over again, saying it to yourself as you write. 2) Write out or type the passage on an index card or piece of paper and attach it to the wall near your desk or on your dresser or bathroom mirror. Recite it to yourself several times each day, as you brush your teeth, get dressed, or wait for your computer to boot up. 3) Put the words to a tune and learn them by singing the tune to yourself.

ADDITIONAL RESOURCES

Bonhoeffer, Dietrich. *Life Together: The Classic Exploration of Faith in Community*. New York: Harper & Row, 1954.

Hestenes, Roberta. *Turning Committees into Communities*. Colorado Springs, CO: NavPress, 1991.

Nouwen, Henri J. M. *The Road to Daybreak*. New York: Image, 1988.

Smith, James Bryan, with Lynda L. Graybeal. *A Spiritual Formation Workbook*. Rev. ed. San Francisco: HarperSanFrancisco, 1999.

Vanier, Jean. *Community and Growth*. Rev. ed. New York: Paulist, 1989.

When in your life have you most closely experienced the community and fellowship of the early Christians?

Is it possible to be a Christian without a faith community?

An integral part of the community of the early Christians was holding possessions in common. How would you react if that were a prerequisite of membership in your church? What does your reaction teach you?

PREACHING THE GOOD NEWS

4

KEY SCRIPTURE: Acts 3:11–26

DEVOTIONAL READING

BRUCE LARSON, *Wind and Fire*

Acts 2:22–40

One of the vital ingredients of the New Testament church was good preaching. That's still an important component of our corporate church life.... Preaching may seem to many an anachronistic art form; yet, there is nothing quite like a good sermon. Unlike books, plays or newspapers, a sermon is a unique means of communicating God's Good News....

Consider the many times in the history of spiritual awakening and renewal that have been associated with the names of great preachers. There was John Wesley in eighteenth century England and in the mid-nineteenth century, there was Charles Finney, the renowned lawyer-turned-preacher. We think of Jonathan Edwards and the Great Awakening in New England, or Dwight Moody, the uneducated layman who became one of the great popular preachers of all time. Farther back, we find preachers like Saint Ignatius of Loyola or Saint Francis of Assisi, who brought the gospel to slaves, pirates and lepers, as well as to kings and princes.

About one hundred and twenty-five years ago, the French government sent the famous sociologist and historian Alexis de Tocqueville to study America and to write an unbiased report on just what makes America so great. He spent several years here, talking to all kinds of people, including leaders in government, business, and the professions. His assay of America filled a great volume, but the conclusion was summed up in this way: "I sought for the greatness and genius of America in her commodious harbors and ample rivers and it was not there. I sought for the greatness and genius of America in her fertile fields and boundless forests, and it was not there. I sought for the greatness

It is helpful for everyone to read the Devotional and Scripture Readings and do the My Life with God Exercise before the meeting. Begin the meeting with silent prayer, then move directly to Reflecting on My Life with God below.

and genius in America in the public school system and her institutions of learning and it was not there. Not until I went into the churches of America and heard her pulpits flame with righteousness, did I understand the secret of her genius and her power." That statement reflects the profound role played by the pulpit message in preserving and continuing the rich heritage received from those who came here with the single desire to worship God in freedom.

What is a good sermon? What do we have a right to expect as God's faithful people occupying the pews? How does Peter's Pentecost sermon help us here?

First of all, a sermon ought to be personal and immediate. It needs to be both specific and incarnational.... A good sermon needs to be relevant. It must answer the questions that are being asked.... A good sermon has a clear purpose.... A good sermon is biblical, grounded in Scripture.... But while a good sermon is scriptural, it is not *about* the Bible. It points to Jesus.... A good sermon uses lots of stories. That was Jesus' own method.... A good sermon is interesting. The ultimate heresy is to make the gospel boring.... A good sermon implies that the preacher is under judgment too.... Finally, a good sermon must offer hope. When the crowd asked Peter what they must do, he said, "Repent and be baptized for the remission of sins, *for the promise is to you and to your children.*"[1]

MY LIFE WITH GOD EXERCISE

Bruce Larson, a Presbyterian pastor and the author and co-author of more than twenty books, not only reminds us that good preaching was at the heart of periods of spiritual awakening and renewals in the Church and at the center of its life in nineteenth-century America, he also suggests that laypeople as well as professionals—ministers, pastors, preachers, evangelists, and priests—should be concerned with discerning whether a sermon is good or bad. He lists ten criteria he feels every sermon should meet—is personal and immediate, is relevant, answers questions being asked, has a clear purpose, is biblical, points to Jesus, uses stories, holds speaker and listeners in judgment, is interesting, and offers hope. As a model, Larson holds up Peter's sermon on the day of Pentecost.

In this exercise, you have two choices. You can either analyze the sermons recorded in the book of Acts using Larson's criteria or ask several questions of yourself as you listen to and reflect on the homily at your home church. Perhaps you will want to try both. Do whatever fits your circumstances and time constraints.

To analyze the sermons, write all of Larson's criteria on the left side of a sheet of paper, then list these scriptural references across the top of the paper: Acts 2:14–41; 3:11–26; 10:34–43; 13:16b–41; 17:22b–31. (For the purposes of this study, we will consider Paul's talk before the Areopagus in Athens a sermon rather than an address.) As you read them, write down the verse or verses that meet Larson's criteria. When you are done, look at the results and ask these questions: Did any sermon meet all of Larson's criteria? Half the criteria? If some met less than half the criteria, what do you think was the reason or reasons? Are some of the criteria more important than others? If so, which ones and why? What value does an exercise like this have for my spiritual formation?

For the other part of the exercise, answer these questions as honestly as you can. What is my normal practice when hearing a homily or sermon? Do I take notes, listen attentively, or find certain points sparking my thoughts to take their own paths? Is the homily a part of the service that I enjoy or that I simply endure? Explore your feelings and attempt to listen to the sermon this week in a different way. If you normally take careful notes, just listen. If you often find your thoughts wandering, attempt to take notes or even outline the homily as it is spoken, then answer these questions: Which of Larson's criteria did the sermon meet? What did I learn from trying to hear the sermon in a different way? How did the Spirit teach me through the homily?

What did you discover about the way you study or experience sermons? How can you better open yourself to the work of the Holy Spirit through this medium?

REFLECTING ON MY
LIFE WITH GOD
Allow each member a few
moments to answer this
question.

➤ SCRIPTURE READING: ACTS 3:11–26

While [the healed beggar] clung to Peter and John, all the people ran together to them in the portico called Solomon's Portico, utterly astonished. When Peter saw it, he addressed the people, "You Israelites, why do you wonder at this, or why do you stare at us, as though by our own power or piety we had made him walk? The God of Abraham, the God of Isaac, and the God of Jacob, the God of our ancestors has glorified his servant Jesus, whom you handed over and rejected in the presence of Pilate, though he had decided to release him. But you rejected the Holy

After everyone has
had a chance to respond
to the question, ask a
member to read this pas-
sage from Scripture.

and Righteous One and asked to have a murderer given to you, and you killed the Author of life, whom God raised from the dead. To this we are witnesses. And by faith in his name, his name itself has made this man strong, whom you see and know; and the faith that is through Jesus has given him this perfect health in the presence of all of you.

"And now, friends, I know that you acted in ignorance, as did also your rulers. In this way God fulfilled what he had foretold through all the prophets, that his Messiah would suffer. Repent therefore, and turn to God so that your sins may be wiped out, so that times of refreshing may come from the presence of the Lord, and that he may send the Messiah appointed for you, that is, Jesus, who must remain in heaven until the time of universal restoration that God announced long ago through his holy prophets. Moses said, 'The Lord your God will raise up for you from your own people a prophet like me. You must listen to whatever he tells you. And it will be that everyone who does not listen to that prophet will be utterly rooted out of the people.' And all the prophets, as many as have spoken, from Samuel and those after him, also predicted these days. You are the descendants of the prophets and of the covenant that God gave to your ancestors, saying to Abraham, 'And in your descendants all the families of the earth shall be blessed.' When God raised up his servant, he sent him first to you, to bless you by turning each of you from your wicked ways."

REFLECTION QUESTION
Allow each person a few moments to respond.

How do you think you might react if you were among those hearing Peter's sermon?

▶▶ GETTING THE PICTURE

↜ After a brief discussion, choose one person to read this section.

Although this sermon and the other four that appear in Acts are the first real examples of this kind of teaching that are recorded in the Bible, preaching as a way of teaching the faithful was not a new concept for Jews. Preaching was already a part of worship in the synagogue; Jesus himself often taught there (see Matt 4:23; Luke 4:16–30; 6:6; John 6:59; 18:20). In the synagogue service any preaching normally followed readings from the law and prophets and was often a commentary on these readings.[2] We see an example of this later in Acts, when Paul and his companions visited the synagogue in Antioch: "And on the sabbath day they went into the synagogue and sat down. After the reading of the law and the prophets, the officials of the synagogue sent them a message, saying, 'Brothers, if you have any word of exhortation for the people, give it.' So Paul stood up and with a gesture began to speak ..." (Acts 13:14b–16a).

In contrast to the Scripture commentary that was typical of sermons in the synagogue, all five sermons in Acts, including the one in our Scripture Reading, emphasize the good news: that Jesus was the Messiah; that he was killed but God raised him from the dead, an event to which the disciples were witnesses; that this was God's plan. Peter also incorporates the need for repentance in the sermon in our Scripture Reading.

It is helpful to remember when studying the sermons in Acts that they were all delivered by Jews converted to the way of Christ and in a mixture of contexts: to Jews and Gentiles, in public place and private home, in religious and irreligious settings. To preach the good news, the apostles take advantage of whatever opportunity presents itself. Just before the events recorded in the Scripture Reading, on one of his trips to worship in the temple, Peter healed a crippled man who was begging at the Beautiful Gate. This catches the attention of the other worshipers, and they run to Solomon's Portico, where the beggar, Peter, and John are, giving Peter the opportunity to tell the crowd the good news of Jesus's life, death, and resurrection.

▶▶▶ GOING DEEPER

Repentance is a constant part of the Christian life, and a central point of Peter's sermon. It is one thing to act in ignorance, but once we know the truth, we should turn our backs on that ignorance and repent. Even though many individuals listening to his sermon did not contribute to the actual trial and crucifixion of Jesus, Peter assumed that each person knew of it and that many approved of what had been done to Jesus by the Roman and Jewish leadership. Indeed, if we search our own hearts, if we consider the initial challenge that a life of discipleship to Jesus can bring us, it is quite possible that many of us would have been right there in Pilate's court, chanting "Crucify him!" No one knew this better than Peter, who himself denied Jesus three times the night Jesus was arrested. In the sermon, Peter advised each person to "repent ... and turn to God so that your sins may be wiped out." The door to God is always open if we are willing to repent.

From Peter's sermon and the other four sermons in Acts, we learn that the good news is simple: Jesus is the Christ who was executed, but God raised him from the dead so that we might enjoy eternal life now

✍ Have another member read this section.

as his friend and be a part of his family forever. Jesus's life is indestructible. If we trust our lives to him, we, too, have indestructible lives. There is no need to make it complicated. And there is no need to worry about how people will respond to that message. The listeners in Acts all responded differently. After the sermon in our Scripture Reading, Peter and John were arrested by Jewish officials for preaching about the resurrection; nonetheless, five thousand people heard their message and believed (4:1–4). How a person responds to the good news is impossible to predict. This fact makes us rely all the more on the action of the Holy Spirit to prepare the ground for the good news and to bring a person to faith in Jesus Christ. Our job is to sow the seed: tell people the good news. Their reactions are in God's hands.

The last thing we learn is that we need not worry about where or when we proclaim the good news; opportunities will present themselves and we should take advantage of them when appropriate. Peter's first sermon, on the day of Pentecost, was evidently in the streets of Jerusalem, and the event recounted in our Scripture Reading was in the temple. Both times Peter seized an opportunity in which attention was already focused on him, in the first story because of the Pentecost spectacle they had just witnessed and in the second instance because of the healing of the beggar. But it is also clear that we need not wait for a sign or wonder. Later we see Peter simply telling a family the good news in their home (Acts 10:34–43). In chapter 13 the apostle Paul proclaims it in a regular Sabbath gathering in a synagogue (16b–43), and later still Luke records that Paul told the good news to bystanders on Mars Hill in Athens, the birthplace of Greek philosophical and intellectual thought (17:22b–31). Peter and Paul proclaimed the gospel in a variety of places to a wide variety of people. With the help of the Holy Spirit, so can we.

REFLECTION QUESTION
Allow each person a few moments to respond.

When have you seized an unexpected opportunity to proclaim the good news? What did you say? What was the result?

▶▶▶▶ POINTING TO GOD

🕊 Choose one member to read this section.

One of the greatest Christian preachers of all time was born John of Antioch in the mid-fourth century in Syria, but is better known by the name he received in honor of his eloquence, John Chrysostom, which means "golden-mouthed." John prepared for a career in the law, but after being baptized at the age of twenty-three, he entered a monastery. He was ordained as a priest in 386 and quickly gained renown for his writings and especially for his powerful sermons, mainly expositions of Scripture. He began to attract huge audiences, often filled with people who previously had been more likely to attend the theater than church.[3] At the age of forty-nine, he was named the bishop of Constantinople. From this powerful position he criticized excessiveness and extreme wealth, angering Empress Eudoxia, who took his words as a personal attack. When charges were brought against him by another church official, the empress was only too happy to rescind his office, but a popular outcry forced her to reinstate him. However, when in one of his sermons he condemned an overly enthusiastic crowd's reaction to a new statue of the empress, she exiled him from Constantinople. Although he no longer had a pulpit, Chrysostom continued to write until his death three years later.

Philip Schaff describes some of the qualities that made Chrysostom's preaching so memorable: "... the fulness of Scripture knowledge, the intense earnestness, the fruitfulness of illustration and application, the variation of topics, the command of language, the elegance and rhythmic flow of his Greek style, the dramatic vivacity, the quickness and ingenuity of his turns, and the magnetism of sympathy with his hearers. He knew how to draw in the easiest manner spiritual nourishment and lessons of practical wisdom from the Word of God, and to make it a divine voice of warning and comfort to every hearer. He was a faithful preacher of truth and righteousness and fearlessly told the whole duty of man.... The effect of his oratory was enhanced by the magnetism of his personality, and is weakened to the reader of a translation or even the Greek original. The living voice and glowing manner are far more powerful than the written and printed letter."[4] This summary highlights just why preaching the good news is still important, even now that we have Jesus's words recorded in the Gospels. When we speak the good news to people, the Holy Spirit is able to work within us and our audience in a powerful way, both to bring the gospel of Jesus Christ to those who have not heard or accepted it and to remind those who are already Christians of its place and power in our lives.

▶▶▶▶ GOING FORWARD

When we think of preaching today, our first thought is the kind of preaching that happens every Sunday in churches around the world. Yet as the sermons in Acts teach us, preaching is not limited to those of

✍ Have another person read this section.

us who have pulpits. Teaching of this sort can occur in homes, on the street, wherever and whenever we are open to listening to the promptings of God. Preaching spreads the good news of Jesus Christ, the good news of God's love; it also serves to instruct and edify us as we try to live the good news. We should each pray not only for an open heart to hear the promptings of the Holy Spirit through the sermons and homilies we hear, but also for the willingness to seize opportunities to share God's good news outside Jesus's Church.

REFLECTION QUESTION
Again, allow each member a few moments to answer this question.

Other than traditional sermons or homilies, what kinds of preaching have you experienced? Which did you find most effective? Why?

✍ After everyone has had a chance to respond, the leader reads this paragraph.

This concludes our look at preaching the good news. In the next chapter we will turn our attention to another avenue of living the mission—being the good news.

✍ **Allow some time for members to encourage one another to read the Devotional and Scripture Readings and do the exercise in the following chapter before the next meeting.** Then invite the members to be silent for a few moments before leading them in reading the Closing Prayer aloud together.

✍ At the end of the Closing Prayer, the leader asks for a volunteer to lead the next meeting.

CLOSING PRAYER

I will extol you, my God and King,
and bless your name forever and ever.
Every day I will bless you,
and praise your name forever and ever.
Great is the LORD, and greatly to be praised;
his greatness is unsearchable.

One generation shall laud your works to another,
and shall declare your mighty acts.
On the glorious splendor of your majesty,
and on your wondrous works, I will meditate.
The might of your awesome deeds shall be proclaimed,
And I will declare your greatness. (PS 145:1–6)

TAKING IT FURTHER

ADDITIONAL EXERCISE

Peter and Paul never hesitated to take an opportunity to preach the good news, even when it seemed as though the message would not be well received. This week be especially watchful for chances to share the good news with those around you.

Chrysostom, John. *On Living Simply*. Liguori, MO: Liguori, 1997.

Larson, Bruce. *Wind and Fire*. Waco, TX: Word, 1984.

White, James F. *The History of Christian Worship*. Nashville, TN: Abingdon, 1993.

What are your criteria for a good sermon?

Why do you think preaching has endured as a way to proclaim the gospel of Jesus Christ?

Which of the five sermons in Acts speaks to you most powerfully? Why?

BEING THE GOOD NEWS

5

DEVOTIONAL READING

ADOMNÁN OF IONA, *Life of St Columba*

Once again while St Columba was living in Iona … he saw a heavy storm-cloud to the north rising from the sea on a clear day. Watching as the cloud rose, Columba turned to one of his monks sitting beside him, a man called Silnán mac Nemaidon, whose people were the moccu Sogin, and said: 'This cloud will bring great harm to people and livestock. Today it will pass over here and tonight it will shed a deadly rain over that part of Ireland between the River Delvin and Dublin, a rain that will raise awful sores full of pus on the bodies of people and on the udders of cattle. All those afflicted with this poisonous infection will suffer a terrible sickness even to death.* But by the mercy of God it is our duty to take pity on them and help them. You, therefore, Silnán, come down with me now from this hill and prepare yourself to set sail tomorrow. For if life continue and God will, you shall take from here bread that I have blessed in the name of God, you shall dip this bread in water and then sprinkle that water over both people and livestock, and they will soon recover health.'

Why do we pause? All necessary preparations were quickly made, and the next day Silnán received from St Columba's hand the bread he had blessed and set sail in peace…. Silnán did as St Columba had said. With the Lord's help his voyage was fair and fast, he landed where the

It is helpful for everyone to read the Devotional and Scripture Readings and do the My Life with God Exercise before the meeting. Begin the meeting with silent prayer, then move directly to Reflecting on My Life with God below.

---

* Retrospective medical diagnosis is never safe, since one does not know what reliance may be placed on the description of the symptoms. A fatal disease, spreading as an epidemic, characterized by pustules, and afflicting cattle as well as humans, would seem to be *variola* (smallpox, cowpox). The symptoms of this disease, and the epidemiology of an outbreak, were probably well known in the Middle Ages and could have been recognized by Adomnán's audience.

saint had said, and found that the population of the district mentioned by St Columba had been wasted by the deadly rain from the cloud that had recently passed over. The first thing to happen was that Silnán found six men in one house by the sea, all close to death. But when he sprinkled them with the water of benediction, within the day they were happily restored to health. Accounts of this sudden cure rapidly circulated throughout the area affected by the disease, and attracted the sick to St Columba's representative, who, in accordance with the saint's command, sprinkled both people and livestock with water in which the blessed bread had been dipped. At once men and beasts regained their health, and praised Christ in St Columba with exceeding gratitude.[1]

MY LIFE WITH GOD EXERCISE

Most of us who have been schooled in the Western tradition of science will look askance at the description of rain from a cloud causing an epidemic and people healed by being sprinkled with water in which blessed bread had been soaked. Events like this do not fit into our understanding of the world around us. We could certainly dismiss this sixth-century tale of St. Columba as apocryphal or highly exaggerated, yet the Gospels and Acts are also filled with stories of signs and wonders. We should not downplay the importance of miracles. The question becomes: What lessons do these stories have for our spiritual formation?

When looking at miracles from this perspective, what stands out in the above story is the reason behind the miracle. When Columba discerned that the cloud would bring suffering to those on whom its rain fell, he said, "But by the mercy of God it is our duty to take pity on them and help them." That pithy sentence summarizes the reason behind all acts of compassion. Just as we learned in the last chapter that we are called to preach the good news, we are also called to be the good news, to reflect Jesus's message in the way we treat those around us. We are meant not only to speak God's word but to show it with our actions, using whatever resources we have at our disposal and trusting that God will assist us with the rest. Columba did not have money, clothing, food, or medicine. All he had was the power of God, so he depended upon that power to help people.

Demonstrating God's love for all people through our actions is no less a responsibility for modern-day Christians. During the next few days, contact your church or a local organization known for its social outreach programs, such as the Salvation Army, and ask where you can help. Other options might be a mentorship organization, such as Big Brothers/Big Sisters of America, a home-building project like those offered by Habitat for Humanity, or a local food bank, soup kitchen, or shelter. Look into several options. Once you have a list, pray over it and ask God to give you the power to be helpful in whatever direction he leads you. Then, as you are led, contact the person responsible for organizing the effort and volunteer to help. This can be a one-time effort or a weekly commitment, whichever feels right and good.

Perhaps you are already committed to many service projects and outreach programs. If so, we ask you to evaluate the compassionate work you are currently doing. Are you utilizing your particular skills and resources? Do you understand your work as being God's good news in the world? Would the people you serve or those who observe you in your role see that in your actions? Consider whether you might be called to serve an additional person or organization regularly or whether you might need to renew or refresh your commitment to a current endeavor. Whether you are working at a new service opportunity or an ongoing one, be sensitive to new ways you might be able to help or other areas that need a person with your abilities and gifts. Remember that whether you are able to see it that way or not, your work being God's good news in the world may represent a miracle to the person or group of people you are helping.

What ways did you find to be God's good news in the world?

REFLECTING ON MY LIFE WITH GOD
Allow each member a few moments to answer this question.

➤ SCRIPTURE READING: LUKE 10:1–11, 17

⤴ After everyone has had a chance to respond to the question, ask a member to read this passage from Scripture.

After this the Lord appointed seventy others and sent them on ahead of him in pairs to every town and place where he himself intended to go. He said to them, "The harvest is plentiful, but the laborers are few; therefore ask the Lord of the harvest to send out laborers into his harvest. Go on your way. See, I am sending you out like lambs into the midst of wolves. Carry no purse, no bag, no sandals; and greet no one on the road. Whatever house you enter, first say, 'Peace to this house!' And if anyone is there who shares in peace, your peace will rest on that person; but if not, it will return to you. Remain in the same house, eating and drinking whatever they provide, for the laborer deserves to be paid. Do not move about from house to house. Whenever you enter a town and its people welcome you, eat what is set before you; cure the sick who are there, and say to them, 'The kingdom of God has come near to you.' But whenever you enter a town and they do not welcome you, go out into its streets and say; 'Even the dust of your town that clings to our feet, we wipe off in protest against you. Yet know this: the kingdom of God has come near.'" ... The seventy returned with joy, saying, "Lord, in your name even the demons submit to us!"

How would you feel if you received these instructions from Jesus?

REFLECTION QUESTION
Allow each person a few moments to respond to this question.

▶▶ GETTING THE PICTURE

After a brief discussion, choose one person to read this section.

In the previous chapter, we discussed the importance of preaching the good news—the reality of Jesus Christ and his message of God's kingdom. Here we find the important second step, that of *being* the good news. Demonstration follows proclamation. Jesus physically sent his disciples out into the world around them to proclaim and to demonstrate the kingdom to those they encountered. As the passage directly preceding our reading states, "Then Jesus called the twelve together and gave them power and authority over all demons and to cure diseases, and he sent them out to proclaim the kingdom of God and to heal.... They departed and went through the villages, bringing the good news and curing diseases everywhere" (9:1–2, 6). Our Scripture Reading contains plenty of very practical advice about just how to proclaim and be the good news: we are advised to work together rather than alone, to rely on God rather than our own money to provide for us, to accept whatever hospitality is offered to us, and more. Underscoring all of this is this wonderful rhythm of verbal announcement of the kingdom of God and physical manifestation of its presence among the People of God.

So what is the purpose of this pattern of proclamation and demonstration? Speculation runs the gamut. Some believe the demonstration validates the teaching; others that it strengthens the faith of followers; others believe it brings people to repentance and trust in Jesus; others cite that it shows God's power over evil, sickness, death, and nature. And those examples touch only a few theories that people glean from the Scriptures (see Matt 11:20–24; Mark 6:1–6; John 5:19; 20:30–31). Whatever the reason, Jesus's and his followers' practice of performing miracles epitomized their "being the good news." Not only were they proclaiming that a new life was available to the people but they were demonstrating it, proving it by their actions. Jesus and his apostles and disciples were meeting the spiritual *and* physical needs of the people. Today we might say that they were not only talking the talk but walking the walk.

As we consider how the above Scripture and the stories from Acts apply to our lives, we learn several things. First, God gives us what we need to proclaim the kingdom of God and to follow up our words with action. Jesus gave specific instructions to the disciples as they went out to prepare the people for his later trip, including telling them not to take purses for money, bags with extra clothing or provisions, or extra pairs of shoes. These instructions underscored that their needs would be taken care of by God. We see that not only their physical needs but also their ability to preach, heal, and make disciples were going to be provided by the Holy Spirit. Likewise, God gives us power through the Holy Spirit to speak words of truth and bring the love of God to a hurting world.

✍ Have another member read this section.

When we learn to rely on God for what we need and follow his guidance, our efforts will bear fruit. The seventy were rejoicing when they got back. That statement implies that perhaps when they left they weren't sure about going, but they followed Jesus's instructions anyway, and their obedience was rewarded when the Holy Spirit helped them demonstrate the good news by performing miracles. We too are often reluctant to get started. When we step out in faith to do something for the kingdom, many times we are unsure about what we are doing or how successful it will be. Even when we are in the middle of the task or effort, we still doubt. Sometimes it takes weeks and even years for us to see our efforts bear fruit. Other times, we may never see the results of our actions, but we must trust that if we are doing our best to follow God's guidance, then our work in the world is indeed producing positive results.

When doing kingdom work, we are to ask the Lord for people to help us. As the Scripture Reading makes clear, this help comes not only in the form of partners in mission, exemplified by the pairs that Jesus sent out, but also in the form of those who will greet us and offer us hospitality, which we are to accept, even perhaps when we feel we do not need it. This is so clear in the Scriptures, yet it is so hard. We tend to be too self-sufficient and too proud to ask for help. It seems we feel like failures if we admit that a job is too big for us or beyond us. Many times we think it is easier to do the job ourselves rather than train someone else to do it. But Jesus clearly trained the seventy to do the same things he was doing and then told them to "ask the Lord of the harvest to send out laborers into his harvest." Columba did not hesitate to recruit Silnán during the epidemic. Neither should we hesitate to ask God for people to help us and trust that he will provide them.

Along these same lines, we are to be gracious to people who befriend us and transparent about what we are doing. Sadly, in our culture Christians do not have a reputation for being gracious to those outside our fellowships. Whether the reputation is earned or not, the general perception is that we are not respectful of people outside our own church or tribe and therefore deserve the many less-than-flattering names that come our way, such as Bible bashers or Bible thumpers. We should be gracious not only to the people who help us, but also to those who ridicule us (see Matt 5:43–47). And there will be those who are not receptive or are downright hostile to our message; Jesus said that he was sending the disciples out as lambs among wolves. He instructed them to proclaim the kingdom even when they were not welcomed, and then move on. Jesus made clear throughout his ministry that we help people, those who are friends and those who are enemies, because we believe that everyone is precious and made in the image of God, and that we are representatives of his kingdom bringing his message of abundant life through our words *and* our actions. Because God has shown us mercy, as St. Columba said, "it is our duty to take pity on them and help them."

REFLECTION QUESTION
Allow each person a few moments to respond.

What part of being God's good news in the world as described in the Scripture Reading do you think you might find the most difficult: accepting the help of a partner in mission, relying on God to provide for your physical needs, trusting in God to provide positive results for your service, or asking for and then accepting help in the form of hospitality, even from those you are serving?

▶▶▶ POINTING TO GOD

Choose one member to read this section.

It is hard to choose just one Christian whose life of service exemplified "being the good news," but one woman who certainly fits the bill is nineteenth-century British prison reformer Elizabeth Fry. Fry, known as the "angel of the prisons," was born into a Quaker family in Norwich, England, in the late eighteenth century. After she married and became a mother, although she remained involved with her local church, she realized that she still felt something was missing in her life, writing in her diary in 1812, "I feel that my life is slipping away to little purpose."[2] In 1813, Stephen Grellet, a family friend, came to her describing the terrible conditions at the women's prison at Newgate. Women prisoners and their children lacked adequate clothing and many times had no beds on which to sleep. Fry immediately enlisted several friends to help her make warm clothing for the babies. Despite warnings from prison workers that the women in the prison were dangerous, she went to visit the prison with her sister-in-law the very next day. There they witnessed for themselves the conditions Grellet had described. Women, some of whom had not even received trials, were crowded together into small cells with nowhere to sleep but the floor. Fry and her sister-in-law brought the clothing they had made and straw bedding for those who were sick; they also prayed for the prisoners. After three visits, Fry was unable to return to the prison for several years because of family troubles, including the death of a daughter.

In late 1816, however, she returned to the prison and, after asking the women what needs they had, decided to start a school. Along with several other women, she formed the Association for the Improvement of the Female Prisoners in Newgate. They started the school; provided materials so that the women prisoners could sew, knit, and bake goods for sale; and visited with and read the Bible to the prisoners. In 1818, Fry was called upon to testify before Parliament about prison conditions, a great honor for a woman, and as a result, associations such as the one in Newgate sprang up all over Britain and Europe. One of the reforms Fry worked for was the hiring of female wardens for female prisoners. She also spoke out on the need for opportunities for women in society in general and started a nurses' training school. Other achievements included starting libraries for coast guards and District Visiting Groups to visit and offer aid to the poor. To this day Elizabeth Fry societies exist to advocate for and support females in the penal system.

▶▶▶▶▶ GOING FORWARD

Fry's life exemplifies being the good news in the world. She immediately sprang into action when Grellet told her about the prison conditions, recognizing that this might be the opportunity to serve God that she had been seeking. Despite the warnings she received about the dangers she might face entering the prison, she went in anyway. She enlisted the help of her friends and family in her prison work, never trying to go it alone. Perhaps Fry was luckier than some of us in that she was able to see the fruit of her labor in the form of the prison reforms she spearheaded, and in the associations that sprang up across Europe.

From Fry's example and the other examples in the chapter, we see the importance of seizing opportunities to follow up our teachings and

✍ Have another person read this section.

our words about being Christian with demonstrations of love. We are called to physically be the good news of Jesus Christ in the world, to serve our fellow people, and to proclaim God's kingdom through deed as well as word. This type of action is the natural outpouring of our commitment to Jesus, a normal outcome of living life with God. As it is said in James 2:26: "For just as the body without the spirit is dead, so faith without works is also dead."

REFLECTION QUESTION
Again, allow each member a few moments to answer this question.

Other than the type of service work discussed in the exercise, how do you seek to act as the good news in the world?

✍ After everyone has had a chance to respond, the leader reads this paragraph.

This concludes our look at being the good news. In the next chapter we will turn our attention to another avenue of living the mission—choosing leaders.

✍ Allow some time for members to encourage one another to read the Devotional and Scripture Readings and do the exercise in the following chapter before the next meeting. Then invite the members to be silent for a few moments before leading them in reading the Closing Prayer aloud together.

✍ At the end of the Closing Prayer, the leader asks for a volunteer to lead the next meeting.

CLOSING PRAYER

I will extol you, my God and King,
    and bless your name forever and ever.
Every day I will bless you,
    and praise your name forever and ever.
Great is the LORD, and greatly to be praised;
    his greatness is unsearchable.

One generation shall laud your works to another,
    and shall declare your mighty acts.
On the glorious splendor of your majesty,
    and on your wondrous works, I will meditate.
The might of your awesome deeds shall be proclaimed,
    And I will declare your greatness. (PS 145:1–6)

TAKING IT FURTHER

ADDITIONAL EXERCISE

Study a biography or autobiography of a historical or contemporary Christian who you feel is an excellent example of being God's good news in the world. Most church libraries contain books about people who were the good news to those around them. Try to learn from their example what it means to demonstrate God's love to the world.

Adomnán of Iona. *Life of St Columba*. Translated by Richard Sharpe.
   New York: Penguin, 1995.
Hatton, Jean. *Betsy: The Dramatic Biography of Prisoner Reformer
   Elizabeth Fry*. Grand Rapids, MI: Kregel, 2006.

In the Scripture Reading, Jesus said he was sending the disciples out like lambs in the midst of wolves. What does this mean to you? Is it true of Christians in the world today?

Jesus directed his disciples to go out into the neighboring towns and proclaim the gospel with no purse and no bag. In what ways or instances in your life have you felt that you were serving Jesus without worldly supplies or support?

What do you believe was the primary reason for the miracles performed throughout the New Testament? What is the place of such miracles in the world and in the Church today?

CHOOSING LEADERS

6

KEY SCRIPTURE: Acts 6:1–6

DEVOTIONAL READING

ROBERT K. GREENLEAF, *Servant Leadership*

Servant and leader—can these two roles be fused in one real person, in all levels of status or calling? If so, can that person live and be productive in the real world of the present? My sense of the present leads me to say yes to both questions....

The idea of *The Servant as Leader** came out of reading Hermann Hesse's *Journey to the East*. In this story we see a band of men on a mythical journey, probably also Hesse's own journey. The central figure of the story is Leo who accompanies the party as the *servant* who does their menial chores, but who also sustains them with his spirit and his song. He is a person of extraordinary presence. All goes well until Leo disappears. Then the group falls into disarray and the journey is abandoned. They cannot make it without the servant Leo. The narrator, one of the party, after some years of wandering finds Leo and is taken into the Order that had sponsored the journey. There he discovers that Leo, whom he had known first as *servant,* was in fact the titular head of the Order, its guiding spirit, a great and noble *leader*....

[T]o me, this story clearly says that *the great leader is seen as servant first,* and that simple fact is the key to his greatness. Leo was actually the leader all of the time, but he was servant first because that was what he was, *deep down inside.* Leadership was bestowed upon a man who was by nature a servant. It was something given, or assumed, that could be taken away. His servant nature was the real man, not bestowed, not assumed, and not to be taken away....

* An essay written prior to *Servant Leadership*.

It is helpful for everyone to read the Devotional and Scripture Readings and do the My Life with God Exercise before the meeting. Begin the meeting with silent prayer, then move directly to Reflecting on My Life with God below.

Who Is the Servant-Leader?

The servant-leader *is* servant first—as Leo was portrayed. It begins with the natural feeling that one wants to serve, to serve *first*. Then conscious choice brings one to aspire to lead. That person is sharply different from one who is *leader* first, perhaps because of the need to assuage an unusual power drive or to acquire material possessions. For such it will be a later choice to serve—after leadership is established. The leader-first and the servant-first are two extreme types. Between them there are shadings and blends that are part of the infinite variety of human nature.

The difference manifests itself in the care taken by the servant-first to make sure that other people's highest priority needs are being served. The best test, and difficult to administer, is: Do those served grow as persons? Do they, *while being served,* become healthier, wiser, freer, more autonomous, more likely themselves to become servants? *And,* what is the effect on the least privileged in society; will they benefit, or, at least, not be further deprived?[1]

MY LIFE WITH GOD EXERCISE

Robert Greenleaf asks a question that is at the heart of this chapter: "Servant and leader—can these two roles be fused in one real person, in all levels of status or calling?" As we consider people for various positions of leadership in our community, we can build on Greenleaf's question in many ways. Do we look for a person who is both a servant and a leader? Or a person who is first a servant? First a leader? How do we choose them? Are they appointed by committees or chosen by the whole fellowship? Or do we just start asking people until someone says yes? Are we sensitive to the spiritual gifts a person has, or do we rely solely on their abilities, as demonstrated in the small business, corporate, educational, or governmental worlds?

We have come to know that one person was able to be the perfect servant and perfect leader at the same time: Jesus Christ. In his epistle to the Philippians, Paul used the words of an early Christian hymn to explain that Jesus, "though he was in the form of God, / did not regard equality with God / as something to be exploited, / but emptied himself, / taking the form of a slave" (2:6–7a). The best earthly example of Jesus the leader functioning in the role of a servant can be found in John 13:3–16. "Jesus, knowing that the Father had given all things into his hands, and that he had come from God and was going to God, got up from the table, took off his outer robe, and tied a towel around himself. Then he poured water into a basin and began to wash the disciples' feet and to wipe them with the towel that was tied around him" (vv 3–5). From studying the life of Jesus, we find that he, like Leo in *Journey to the East,* was first the servant, as Greenleaf writes, *"deep down inside."* Jesus's act of washing his disciples' feet exemplified the way he served people in his life: healing, teaching, defending, blessing, and ultimately dying for them.

Trying to determine where we are on the continuum of servant to leader is tricky and subjective because, as Greenleaf writes, "Between [the extremes] are shadings and blends that are part of the infinite variety of human nature." Perhaps the place to start is how you view yourself. Are you a servant or a leader or someplace in between? Then think about people you know who are servants. What are the qualities that make them a servant? How are these qualities expressed? Then think about the same questions for people you know who are leaders. Do you know of anyone who you can truly call a servant-leader? If so, what sets them apart? Then, ask a few of the people you know well, "Do you see me more as a servant or more as a leader (or more as neither!)?"

Next, try doing one action typical of servants and one action typical of leaders. Servant activities could include cleaning up the kitchen, getting a meal for your family, volunteering to serve food at a fellowship function, doing the laundry, running errands for a shut-in, encouraging a depressed person, babysitting for a neighbor. Leader activities could include chairing a committee, thinking of a new ministry your church could do and presenting it to the governing board, or even initiating and organizing an event or party for your fellowship or group of friends. Obviously, finding and doing servant activities is easier than functioning as a leader—which is convenient since there are very few of us who couldn't benefit from more opportunities to be a servant, even if we naturally gravitate to such a role. Perhaps your answers to the questions will help you think of servant-leader actions that you can incorporate into your life in either the short or long term. Pay attention to the way you feel about acting as a servant and as a leader. It will likely be very clear which role is more natural and comfortable to you. To become servant-leaders, we all must work to develop the role with which we feel less comfortable.

What insights did you gain about servants and leaders? Where do you think you fall between the extremes of servant-first and leader-first?

▶ SCRIPTURE READING: ACTS 6:1–6

✎ After everyone has had a chance to respond to the question, ask a member to read this passage from Scripture.

Now during those days, when the disciples were increasing in number, the Hellenists complained against the Hebrews because their widows were being neglected in the daily distribution of food. And the twelve called together the whole community of disciples and said, "It is not right that we should neglect the word of God in order to wait on tables. Therefore, friends, select from among yourselves seven men of good standing, full of the Spirit and of wisdom, whom we may appoint to this task, while we, for our part, will devote ourselves to prayer and to serving the word." What they said pleased the whole community, and they chose Stephen, a man full of faith and the Holy Spirit, together with Philip, Prochorus, Nicanor, Timon, Parmenas, and Nicolaus, a proselyte of Antioch. They had these men stand before the apostles, who prayed and laid their hands on them.

Name one thing that stands out to you in this Scripture.

REFLECTION QUESTION
Allow each person a few moments to respond to this question.

▶▶ GETTING THE PICTURE

✎ After a brief discussion, choose one person to read this section.

From our Scripture Reading we learn of a challenge the early Church faced from within, most likely resulting from its rapid growth and the number of poor who were attracted by the message the apostles were proclaiming. Hellenist widows are being neglected during the daily distribution of food. The apostles had learned from Jesus that they should care for the poor (see Mark 10:21), so they developed a practice of distributing food to the needy, but someone was apparently overlooking this particular group. This is the first time a cultural difference among the disciples becomes an issue in the life of the Church.

The Hellenist widows had two obstacles to overcome: their ethnicity and their marital status. Opinions vary as to who the Hellenists were. Some regard them as Greek-speaking Jews who did not follow the law as strictly as Aramaic-speaking Jews. Others think they were Jews who grew up in the diaspora*, were fluent in Greek, and lived according to Greek ways, as opposed to Jews who grew up in the Roman provinces of Galilee and Judea, spoke Aramaic, and lived according to Jewish ways. It is likely that at least some of the reason the Hellenist widows were not

---

* The dispersion of the Jews outside the land of Palestine after the Babylonian exile in 586 BC.

being given their share of food was because of prejudice from the majority group of Aramaic-speaking Hebrews. Furthermore, even though provisions had been made in the Mosaic law for widows, and the Israelites had been taught that their neglect or oppression provoked divine judgment (see Exod 22:22–24; Job 22:9–11; Ps 94:1–7; Isa 1:16–17, 21–25), the financial position of widows was precarious both in ancient Israel and in the first century. They had no means of support if their sons died before them. Their daughters could not help them because once they married, they were considered to belong to their husband's family rather than their family of origin.

The twelve apostles call together the entire community of disciples to consider this problem, and the community as a whole chooses the seven men listed to solve the problem at hand. At least one of the men chosen, Stephen, was himself a Hellenist, and possibly all seven belonged to this minority.

▶▶▶ GOING DEEPER

This Scripture Reading shows us that being sensitive to an issue in our community and taking action is the hallmark of a servant-leader. The apostles were sensitive to what was happening among the disciples sitting under their instruction. Nothing is said about how they learned of the problem, who brought the issue to their attention, or if one of them investigated the complaints. Luke simply writes, "The Hellenists complained against the Hebrews" (v 1). It would have been easy to dismiss the complaint as frivolous or trivial. Instead the apostles chose to call "together the whole community of the disciples." The issue was confronted quickly and action taken to alleviate the dispute.

✍ Have another member read this section.

The servant-leader knows his or her calling and stays within it. The apostles knew that their duty was to devote themselves "to prayer and to serving the word," not to wait on tables. Waiting on tables was not beneath their dignity; it was simply not a part of their calling. So they gathered the whole community together to let them discern who among their number had the calling of waiting on tables. Now, it may seem unreasonable in our time to involve the entire fellowship in naming people to areas of service like taking meals to the poor. One might argue that it would be a waste of everyone's time. There is, however, a compelling argument for it: the presence and power of the Holy Spirit is stronger when the community is gathered to seek an answer to issues that affect the entire fellowship.

The apostles enumerate three criteria that our communities can use when choosing leaders: they should be "of good standing, full of the Spirit, and wise" (v 3). Again, these can seem unreasonable in our community, where we may have difficulty recruiting people to fill all of the positions, from small group leaders to governing body members. It makes sense, however, in the long term. It reflects on the community as a whole if a leader exercises poor judgment; further, it could have terrible consequences for those under that person's leadership. And it goes without saying that being in tune with the Holy Spirit should be a non-negotiable quality of our leaders. The last criteria for a leader, wisdom, is more than just knowledge; it encompasses knowledge, common sense, and supernatural wisdom, all of which are used for kingdom purposes. How many problems could be eliminated if we followed these criteria when choosing leaders?

REFLECTION QUESTION
Allow each person a few moments to respond.

What would it look like for your church to follow similar guidelines when choosing leaders?

▶▶▶▶ POINTING TO GOD

✍ Choose one member to read this section.

Many of us may read about how the early church chose its leaders and shake our heads, thinking that such a thing couldn't possibly be replicated in our own churches for whatever reason. But one denomination, the Religious Society of Friends, or Quakers, is known for the process of discernment by which they choose leaders. All such decisions are made at a monthly "meeting for worship with a concern for business." The title is deliberate, as it is meant to emphasize that any decisions made at such meetings are made with the aid of the Holy Spirit. Instead of debating and voting, Friends are expected to listen for the will of God on any given issue and, if so led, to share their insights with the group as a whole. The goal is to "wait upon the Lord" until everyone gathered is in agreement about the way to proceed, with the understanding that when a mutual decision is reached, it will match the Lord's will. This is called "coming to unity." If a mutual decision cannot be reached, then the Clerk says, "We are not of one mind," and the business is left uncompleted. At times one or more members can choose to "stand aside" if they do not find themselves in agreement but are willing to let the decision move forward.

A newsletter sums up the ground rules for the process Quakers use to choose leaders: "Proceed in the peaceable spirit of the light of Truth, with forbearance and warm affection for each other. Be willing to wait upon God as long as may be necessary for the emergence of a decision which clearly recommends itself as the right one. Feel free to express views, but refrain from pressing them unduly. Guard against contentiousness, obstinacy and love of power. Admit the possibility of being in error. In Meetings for Business, and in all duties connected with them, seek the leadings of the Light."[2] An important assumption underlying this entire process is the Friends' longstanding belief that all people are created equal by God, and thus each person's opinion and insight is of equal value.

►►►►► GOING FORWARD

The action of the early Church in choosing people to wait on tables, as recorded in the Scripture Reading, established a precedent that later became a formal position of leadership: the deacon (see Rom 16:1; Phil 1:1; 1 Tim 3:8–13). Many denominations today have retained this leadership role and its focus on the welfare of church members and that of society at large. The deacon role, then and in many denominations now, is truly an example of servant-leadership. Deacons are leaders within the church and are chosen accordingly, but their work is often menial and underappreciated: mowing church lawns, shoveling snow, seeing to building maintenance, organizing community work days, assessing church outreach efforts, and researching ways to be of assistance. Because of Jesus's example, not only the roles of deacons but every leadership role within the church should be filled by a servant-leader, someone whose main focus is the welfare of those around him or her and who is not afraid to do thankless, unglamorous tasks even if they go unnoticed. "A true leader makes 'every decision based on other people,'" said Sharon Miner, the director of a leadership group in Texas.[3] This is one reason why choosing our leaders is such an important task.

Have another person read this section.

The Scripture Reading teaches us the importance of choosing leadership in an intentional and participatory way. For the apostles, this meant bringing the matter before the entire group of disciples. We all know that choosing leaders can sow a great deal of discord among church members. At times there is disagreement about who the best candidate is; at other times we despair of even finding someone to fill a certain position. One key lesson we can learn from both the early church and the modern example of the Quakers is the Holy Spirit–guided process of discernment that takes place when as much of the fellowship as possible is present and committed to achieving unity and consensus before a final decision is made. Of course, the Holy Spirit can also lead through other types of authority, such as committees or the decision of a single leader, but a fellowship "coming to unity" is an ideal that can be realized in practice.

REFLECTION QUESTION
Again, allow each member a few moments to answer this question.

What examples have you seen of a larger, more representative group being able to discern better than a smaller, elite group?

After everyone has had a chance to respond, the leader reads this paragraph.

This concludes our look at choosing leaders. In the next chapter we will turn our attention to another avenue of living the mission—making disciples.

Allow some time for members to encourage one another to read the Devotional and Scripture Readings and do the exercise in the following chapter before the next meeting. Then invite the members to be silent for a few moments before leading them in reading the Closing Prayer aloud together.

At the end of the Closing Prayer, the leader asks for a volunteer to lead the next meeting.

CLOSING PRAYER

I will extol you, my God and King,
    and bless your name forever and ever.
Every day I will bless you,
    and praise your name forever and ever.
Great is the LORD, and greatly to be praised;
    his greatness is unsearchable.

One generation shall laud your works to another,
    and shall declare your mighty acts.
On the glorious splendor of your majesty,
    and on your wondrous works, I will meditate.
The might of your awesome deeds shall be proclaimed,
    And I will declare your greatness. (PS 145:1–6)

TAKING IT FURTHER

ADDITIONAL EXERCISE

Choose the person you know, from your fellowship, workplace, or circle of acquaintances, who you feel best exemplifies the ideal of the servant-leader, and talk with him or her. Explain that you consider her or him to be an example of a servant-leader and explain why. Ask whether they consider themselves to be a servant first or a leader first, and how they were able to develop the characteristics that came less naturally. Finally, ask them for any insight they might have for you to develop either your servant or leader side, whichever you feel is lacking.

Greenleaf, Robert K. *Servant Leadership*. New York: Paulist, 1977.

Trueblood, D. Elton. *The People Called Quakers*. Richmond, IN: Friends United Press, 1985.

Young, David. *Servant Leadership for Church Renewal: Shepherds by the Living Springs*. Scottdale, PA: Herald, 1999.

ADDITIONAL RESOURCES

What leadership positions have you held in your life? Within your church? If you haven't held any positions of leadership in your church, what do you think is holding you back?

ADDITIONAL REFLECTION QUESTIONS

It is often said that in churches and many other organizations as well, 10 percent of the people do 90 percent of the work. Is that true of your church? If so, should it look differently? Is there anything you could do to change the situation?

What kind of servant opportunities present themselves in your life each day?

MAKING DISCIPLES

7

KEY SCRIPTURE: Acts 6:7–8

DEVOTIONAL READING

MAX LUCADO, *Just Like Jesus*

What if, for one day, Jesus were to become you?

What if, for twenty-four hours, Jesus wakes up in your bed, walks in your shoes, lives in your house, assumes your schedule? Your boss becomes his boss, your mother becomes his mother, your pains become his pains? With one exception, nothing about your life changes. Your health doesn't change. Your circumstances don't change. Your schedule isn't altered. Your problems aren't solved. Only one change occurs.

What if, for one day and one night Jesus lives your life with his heart? Your heart gets the day off, and your life is led by the heart of Christ. His priorities govern your actions. His passions drive your decisions. His love directs your behavior.

What would you be like? Would people notice a change? Your family—would they see something new? Your coworkers—would they sense a difference? What about the less fortunate? Would you treat them the same? And your friends? Would they detect more joy? How about your enemies? Would they receive more mercy from Christ's heart than from yours?

And you? How would you feel? What alterations would this transplant have on your stress level? Your mood swings? Your temper? Would you sleep better? Would you see sunsets differently? Death differently? Taxes differently? Any chance you'd need fewer aspirin or sedatives? How about your reaction to traffic delays? (Ouch, that touched a nerve.) Would you still dread what you are dreading? Better yet, would you still do what you are doing?

Would you still do what you planned to do for the next twenty-four hours? Pause and think about your schedule. Obligations. Engagements.

It is helpful for everyone to read the Devotional and Scripture Readings and do the My Life with God Exercise before the meeting. Begin the meeting with silent prayer, then move directly to Reflecting on My Life with God below.

Outings. Appointments. With Jesus taking over your heart, would anything change? . . .

God's plan for you is nothing short of a new heart. If you were a car, God would want control of your engine. If you were a computer, God would claim the software and hard drive. If you were an airplane, he'd take his seat in the cockpit. But you are a person, so God wants to change your heart.

"But you were taught to be made new in your hearts, to become a new person. That new person is made to be like God—made to be truly good and holy" (Eph. 4:23–24).

God wants you to be just like Jesus. He wants you to have a heart like his.

I'm going to risk something here. It's dangerous to sum up grand truths in one statement, but I'm going to try. If a sentence or two could capture God's desire for each of us, it might read like this:

> God loves you just the way you are, but he refuses to leave you that way. He wants you to be just like Jesus.[1]

MY LIFE WITH GOD EXERCISE

In chapter 1 we learned that the mission given by Jesus to the disciples was to "go therefore and *make disciples* of all nations, baptizing them in the name of the Father and of the Son and of the Holy Spirit, and teaching them to obey everything that I have commanded you" (Matt 28:19–20a, emphasis added). Their mission was not to save souls, which is God's business, but to make disciples of Jesus Christ who would then make disciples of Jesus Christ who would then make disciples of Jesus Christ, and so on. And what is a disciple of Jesus Christ? It is a person who imitates him. It is a person who does what Jesus did, reacts like Jesus did when he strode the earth in human form. Dallas Willard expresses it this way: "A disciple, or apprentice, is simply someone who has decided to be with another person, under appropriate conditions, in order to become capable of doing what that person does or to become what that person is."[2] In the Devotional Reading, Max Lucado expresses this reality by likening discipleship to seeking to have Jesus's heart.

As an experiment in becoming a disciple and making a disciple, find a friend or two to do this exercise with you. Once you have one or more companions, get together and read **out loud** the Sermon on the Mount, found in Matthew 5–7. You may want to read it more than once, with a different person reading each time so that all have the opportunity to only listen, to hear it as a true sermon. Try to forget every explanation of or debate about the beatitudes and the other subjects Jesus talks about. Read it with fresh eyes with the idea that it addressed ordinary people with everyday problems and issues in their lives, that it describes the kind of life in which we eventually and naturally fulfill the laws of God. If your Bible has subheads, pay no attention to them. Just read it.

After you have finished reading and had a chance to reflect in silence and conversation, each person should pick a topic from Jesus's teaching, one that touches on a personal weakness. Perhaps one of you has a problem with lust, objectifying others for your own sexual imaginings. Or someone finds it difficult to want the best for an adversary or enemy. Or a member of your group tends to be judgmental and critical of others.

Whichever specific teaching in Jesus's sermon speaks to you individually, commit to one another that the very next day you will get up early and reread the Sermon on the Mount and then for the next twelve to fourteen hours be uncommonly aware of the area of difficulty Jesus's preaching identified, be it lusting, loving an enemy, being judgmental, getting angry, lying, or another area. Live this day especially attuned to this shortcoming and do your best to—as Max Lucado describes in the Devotional Reading—live your life as though Jesus had taken it over, at least in this one area. You may want to reread the above selection from Lucado to prepare for the day or to refocus yourself halfway through the day. The goal is not to be perfect on the outside in action, but to be intentionally aware of your failing and to monitor your heart as the day goes on, inviting God to change it. In so doing you are opening yourself to Jesus's transformative teaching.

If you can, meet that evening to reflect together on your experience. You will be helping one another be better disciples of Jesus.

What happened when you spent a day trying to behave as though Jesus were you? Did the results inspire you to try to continue the process?

REFLECTING ON MY LIFE WITH GOD
Allow each member a few moments to answer this question.

➤ **SCRIPTURE READING:** ACTS 6:7–8

The word of God continued to spread; the number of the disciples increased greatly in Jerusalem, and a great many of the priests became obedient to the faith. Stephen, full of grace and power, did great wonders and signs among the people.

🖎 After everyone has had a chance to respond to the question, ask a member to read this passage from Scripture.

REFLECTION QUESTION
Allow each person a few
moments to respond to
this question.

Why do you think so many became disciples so quickly?

After a brief discus-
sion, choose one person
to read this section.

➤➤ GETTING THE PICTURE

In Acts 6:1 we read that "the disciples were increasing in number." In the verses quoted above, Luke writes that "the number of disciples increased greatly." To make almost the same statement twice within such a short space gives added weight to its importance and indicates that the apostles were living the mission that Jesus had given them—to "make disciples"—and that these new disciples were carrying the mission forward by making more disciples. And "the word of God continued to spread." As we learned in chapter 4, this word of God was the message that Jesus was the Messiah, that he lived, died, and came back to life. Implicit in that statement is the fact that Jesus introduced a new kind of life, a life radically different from the one people had come to expect.

This was at the heart of Jesus's teaching from the beginning of his ministry. And many people were ready for a different way. The Jews had been taught to follow the Mosaic law, but various groups in Judaism—Sadducees, Pharisees, priests, scribes, and specialists within those groups—interpreted the law differently. One group would tell the Israelites to do one thing, and another would tell them to do something else. In addition, the religious leaders did not have answers for all of the difficulties they confronted. Faced with these religious challenges and the difficulties of living under Roman occupation, people were searching for answers. We see this in the crowds that flocked to hear John the Baptist's message of repentance and baptism. It is apparent in the number of people who hung on Jesus's every word and the way his disciples responded to the parables and stories. For the most part, the people who sat down to hear Jesus talk were just like you and me. They faced daily the same kinds of problems we face: disagreements with a spouse, anger at a neighbor, disputes over fair charges for labor, failed business ventures, the impulse to not tell the full truth or to embellish a story. These are the people and the issues Jesus addressed.

In the Sermon on the Mount (Matt 5–7), for example, Jesus did not tell his listeners what they were doing wrong or condemn them. He was not advocating external laws that put a nice veneer over a rotten interior, but a life—a life that was transformed from the inside out. Over and over Jesus emphasized that external attempts to control behavior were hopeless. He said in Matthew 23:25–26: "You clean the outside of the cup and of the plate, but inside [you] are full of greed and self-indulgence.... First clean the inside of the cup, so that the outside also may become clean." When Jesus, the representative of the kingdom that is here among them, described a life that the apostle Paul later described as being filled with "love, joy, peace, patience, kindness, generosity, faithfulness, gentleness, and self-control" (Gal 5:22–23), people came from far and near.

This is the word of God, the message the apostles proclaim, which increases the number of disciples by leaps and bounds. They instill in their listeners the vision of the kind of life Jesus described. Once these new disciples become part of the fellowship the apostles teach them the fine points that were broadly outlined in the sermons (see chapter 4). From the amount of Scripture quoted in books written by the apostles, we can imagine that they quoted extensively from the Hebrew Scriptures in order to help the new converts understand their role in the story of God's people. We do not know how long a person sat under the instruction of the apostles in the early Church before they were able to proclaim the good news themselves and in turn make disciples. Likely then, as now, it took different amounts of time for different people, since discipleship is a process. We do know that once churches were organized, "Those who were taught the word must share all good things with their teacher" (Gal 6:6).

▶▶▶ GOING DEEPER

From the four phrases in the Scripture Reading we learn several important insights. "The word of God continued to spread." We can never downplay the extraordinary power of the word of God to make disciples. Those who have been given the spiritual gifts of evangelism, prophecy, teaching, and exhortation speak the *debar Yahweh,* the word of God, to our souls. Theirs is not a small responsibility. Under the power and guidance of the Holy Spirit their words guide us and chide us into a closer walk with the Word of God made flesh, Jesus Christ, as we continue to imitate him or, as Max Lucado describes, his heart becomes our heart. And even with the complete scriptural canon to aid us, we still need the *Kol Yahweh,* the living voice of God. As the eighteenth-century Anglican writer William Law said, "To say that because we now have all the writings of Scripture complete we no longer need the miraculous inspiration

⤴ Have another member read this section.

of Spirit among men as in former days, is a degree of blindness as great as any that can be charged upon the scribes and Pharisees."[3]

"The number of the disciples increased greatly in Jerusalem." There is always room for more disciples in the kingdom of God. The first apostles and disciples could have decided to quit proclaiming the word of God when the room they were meeting in became full, or they could have decided to limit the number of converts. Exclusivity is a great temptation, but the disciples did not give in to it. Instead they continued to go to the temple to worship, where they met people and talked to them about this carpenter from Galilee, Jesus of Nazareth, who taught that there was more to life than following the rules and trying to be good; that they could be changed from the inside out; that this same Jesus rose from the dead to prove that his words were true; that this abundant life was available to them right now, right here. Wouldn't it be wonderful if we could honestly say, "The number of disciples has increased greatly in my town this year"?

"And a great many of the priests became obedient to the faith." All of us need to commit to being a disciple of Christ, even those of us who are spiritual leaders. Many times those of us in positions of leadership in our churches are also spiritually blind and needy. Those of us who are pastors, in particular, know that it is possible to hold a high position in a church or have a lofty theological education and still not know the ways and life of Jesus Christ. Position and education are nothing if we are not apprenticed to Jesus Christ. The Israelite priests who were becoming obedient to the faith came from the Levites, a priestly class who had access to education and privileges unavailable to the ordinary person on the street. They were the equivalent of clergy in affluent churches today. But despite their education in the ways of God and their connections in the temple, just like us, the Israelite priests then and pastors now still need to accept Jesus's offer of "life, and life more abundantly" (John 10:10b).

"Stephen, full of grace and power, did great wonders and signs among the people." Not only is there always room for more people in the kingdom of God, but gifts of the Holy Spirit are distributed regardless of ethnicity. As we learned in chapter 6, Stephen was a Hellenist and therefore out of the mainstream of Jewish life. That didn't matter to God, who gives "the manifestation of the Spirit for the common good" (1 Cor 12:7). Stephen was able to do "great wonders" to confirm God's continual presence within the community and to draw more people into their circle and hence into the kingdom. Stephen was blessed by God when he received the spiritual gifts, but the community and new disciples who came to

God after seeing the lame walk and the blind see received much more. So we too may have witnessed God's signs and wonders and be able to attest to their power to attract potential disciples to the kingdom.

In Going Deeper, we speculated that the disciples could have stopped making disciples when their meeting room became too full. What could be some reasons today why we might hesitate to make more disciples?

REFLECTION QUESTION
Allow each person a few moments to respond.

▶▶▶▶ POINTING TO GOD

Someone who excelled at making disciples was Benedict of Nursia, who is generally acknowledged as the founder of Western monasticism. Benedict was born in the fifth century in Italy; at a young age he left the busy life of Rome and became a hermit for three years. He went on to found thirteen monasteries in the valley of Subiaco and served as the father or abbot of all. When it became clear to Benedict that the monks under his charge needed some guidelines to help them live together as disciples, he created his famous Rule of St. Benedict.

✍ Choose one member to read this section.

The Rule consists of seventy-three chapters in which are set forth the duties of the abbot, the rules about worship in the community, discipline and penal regulations, administrative policies, and other miscellaneous regulations. In the preface he declares the main purpose of the religious life to be the renunciation of self and the "taking up of arms under the banner of Christ."[4] He saw the monastery as a school in which disciples might learn enough to take part in Christ's kingdom. Some of the regulations are as specific as stating that each monk must have his own bed and sleep in his habit in order to be ready to rise quickly for morning prayers, or limiting meals to two a day; others are more general, such as recommending humility, charity, reverence, and moderation in the use of speech, or calling for the just distribution of any private possessions. But probably the best-known part of the Rule sets out the Divine Office—the hours and orders of the various prayers and worship services held throughout the day. Benedict understood that attention to the details of life large and small is an essential part of maintaining discipleship. Kathleen Norris writes, "Benedict knows that practicalities—the order and times for psalms to be read, care of tools, the amount and type of food and drink and clothing—are also spiritual concerns. Many communal ventures begun with high hopes have foundered over the question of who takes out the garbage. Over and over the Rule calls us to be mindful of the little things, even as it reminds us of the big picture, allowing us a glimpse of who we can be when we remember to love. Benedict insists that this remembering is hard work needing daily attention and care.... 'No one shall be excused from kitchen duty,' Benedict says.... Today that means that the Benedictine scholar with the Ph.D. scrubs pots and pans alongside a confrere who has an eighth-grade education, the dignified abbot or abbess dishes out food and washes refectory tables after the meal."[5]

>>>>> GOING FORWARD

↪ Have another person read this section.

To be a disciple means changing the way we live our everyday lives. What we do with our time. What we do with our money. With whom we spend our time. On whom and what we spend our money. Time. Money. People. We interact with these three constantly. It is through them that we encourage our own discipleship and nurture the discipleship of others. We learn this from the early Christian community, which intentionally gathered together for the breaking of bread, the saying of prayers, the hearing of the word, the caring for one another. We learn this from Benedict and those following the tradition he founded, which involves intentionally gathering together for cooking, praying, cleaning, studying. These are the ways the early Christians and the Benedictines helped one another be Jesus's disciples. We can do the same for one another in our everyday lives, by intention and grace.

It is in the evidence of our everyday lives that we find confirmation that we are helping one another along the path of discipleship. As we fill ourselves with the word of God and arm ourselves with the Holy Spirit, whom do we become? If we set out to make ourselves as much like Christ as we can be, how are we seen by those around us? May it be as those in the early Church were viewed by their contemporaries. As religion scholar Huston Smith said, "The people who heard Jesus' disciples proclaiming the Good News were as impressed by what they saw as by what they heard. They saw lives that had been transformed—men and women who were ordinary in every way except for the fact that they seemed to have found the secret of living. They evinced a tranquility, simplicity and cheerfulness that their hearers had nowhere else encountered. Here were people who seemed to be making a success of the enterprise everyone would like to succeed at—life itself."[6] May we, with God's help, evidence the same transformed lives, so we can make numerous other disciples of Jesus Christ.

In what ways were you helped to become a disciple of Jesus Christ? In what ways have you helped someone else?

This concludes our look at making disciples. At the next meeting we will turn our attention to another avenue of living the mission—experiencing persecution.

CLOSING PRAYER

I will extol you, my God and King,
　　and bless your name forever and ever.
Every day I will bless you,
　　and praise your name forever and ever.
Great is the Lord, and greatly to be praised;
　　his greatness is unsearchable.

One generation shall laud your works to another,
　　and shall declare your mighty acts.
On the glorious splendor of your majesty,
　　and on your wondrous works, I will meditate.
The might of your awesome deeds shall be proclaimed,
　　And I will declare your greatness. (PS 145:1–6)

TAKING IT FURTHER

- Together with a friend or group of friends, try to create your own Rule, similar to the one created by Benedict. What parts of life would you focus on? What small details would you find most important?

- Consider making a visit to or planning a short stay at a monastery, Benedictine or otherwise, where the Rule is practiced. Seek to learn how following a Rule can help us be better disciples by following God in the tiniest parts of everyday life.

ADDITIONAL EXERCISES

Lucado, Max. *Just Like Jesus*. Nashville, TN: Word, 1998.
Norris, Kathleen. *The Cloister Walk*. New York: Riverhead, 1996.
Smith, James Bryan, with Lynda L. Graybeal. *A Spiritual Formation Workbook*. Rev. ed. San Francisco: HarperSanFrancisco, 1999.
De Waal, Esther. *Seeking God: The Way of St. Benedict*. Collegeville, MN: Liturgical Press, 2001.

ADDITIONAL RESOURCES

If we are brutally honest with ourselves, we see that our disciple-making might be hampered because we do not necessarily want everyone to belong to our "club" of Christianity. How do you see this tendency in your own life?

Reflecting on Huston Smith's quote about the example of the transformed lives of the early Christians, what do you think visitors to your fellowship would see?

Can you imagine yourself living in a community as carefully regulated as a Benedictine monastery? Why or why not?

LIVING THE MISSION

EXPERIENCING PERSECUTION

8

KEY SCRIPTURE: Acts 6:8–15; 7:51–8:4

DEVOTIONAL READING

J. C. ROBERTSON, "Tertullian, Perpetua and Companions (A.D. 181–206)"

After more than twenty years of peace, there were cruel persecutions in some places, under the reign of Severus. The most famous of the martyrs who then suffered were Perpetua and her companions, who belonged to the same country with Tertullian, and perhaps to his own city, Carthage. Perpetua was a young married lady, and had a little baby only a few weeks old. Her father was a heathen, but she herself had been converted, and was a "catechumen"—which was the name given to converts who had not yet been baptized, but were in a course of "catechising," or training for baptism. When Perpetua had been put into prison, her father went to see her, in the hope that he might persuade her to give up her faith. "Father," she said, "you see this vessel standing here; can you call it by any other than its right name?" He answered, "No." "Neither," said Perpetua, "can I call myself anything else than what I am—a Christian." On hearing this, her father flew at her in such anger that it seemed as if he would tear out her eyes; but she stood so quietly that he could not bring himself to hurt her, and he went away and did not come again for some time.

In the meanwhile Perpetua and some of her companions were baptized; and at her baptism she prayed for grace to bear whatever sufferings might be in store for her. The prison in which she and the others were shut up was a horrible dungeon, where Perpetua suffered much from the darkness, the crowded state of the place, the heat and closeness of the air, and the rude behaviour of the guards. But most of all she was distressed about her poor little child, who was separated from her, and was pining away. Some kind Christians, however, gave money to

✍ It is helpful for everyone to read the Devotional and Scripture Readings and do the My Life with God Exercise before the meeting. Begin the meeting with silent prayer, then move directly to Reflecting on My Life with God below.

the keepers of the prison, and got leave for Perpetua and her friends to spend some hours of the day in a lighter part of the building, where her child was brought to see her. And after a while she took him to be always with her, and then she felt as cheerful as if she had been in a palace.

The martyrs were comforted by dreams, which served to give them courage and strength to bear their sufferings, by showing them visions of blessedness which was to follow. When the day was fixed for their trial, Perpetua's father went again to see her. He begged her to take pity on his old age, to remember all his kindness to her, and how he had loved her best of all his children. He implored her to think of her mother and her brothers, and of the disgrace which would fall on all the family if she were to be put to death as an evil-doer. The poor old man shed a flood of tears; he humbled himself before her, kissing her hands, throwing himself at her feet, and calling her Lady instead of Daughter. But, although Perpetua was grieved to the heart, she could only say, "God's pleasure will be done on us. We are not in our own power, but in His."

One day, as the prisoners were at dinner, they were suddenly hurried off to their trial. The market-place, where the judge was sitting, was crowded with people, and when Perpetua was brought forward, her father crept as close to her as he could, holding out her child, and said, "Take pity on your infant." The judge himself entreated her to pity the little one and the old man, and to sacrifice but, painful as the trial was, she steadily declared that she was a Christian, and that she could not worship false gods. At these words, her father burst out into such loud cries that the judge ordered him to be put down from the place where he was standing and to be beaten with rods. Perhaps the judge did not mean so much to punish the old man for being noisy as to try whether the sight of his suffering might not move his daughter; but, although Perpetua felt every blow as if it had been laid upon herself, she knew that she must not give way. She was condemned, with her companions, to be exposed to wild beasts; and, after she had been taken back to prison, her father visited her once more. He seemed as if beside himself with grief; he tore his white beard, he cursed his old age, and spoke in a way that might have moved a heart of stone. But still Perpetua could only be sorry for him; she could not give up her Saviour.

The prisoners were kept for some time after their condemnation, that they might be put to death at some great games which were to be held on the birthday of one of the emperor's sons; and during this confinement their behaviour had a great effect on many who saw it. The gaoler himself was converted by it, and so were others who had gone to

LIVING THE MISSION

gaze at them. At length the appointed day came, and the martyrs were led into the amphitheatre. The men were torn by leopards and bears; Perpetua and a young woman named Felicitas, who had been a slave, were put into nets and thrown before a furious cow, who tossed them and gored them cruelly; and when this was over, Perpetua seemed as if she had not felt it, but were awaking from a trance, and she asked when the cow was to come. She then helped Felicitas to rise from the ground, and spoke words of comfort and encouragement to others. When the people in the amphitheatre had seen as much as they wished of the wild beasts, they called out that the prisoners should be killed. Perpetua and the rest then took leave of each other, and walked with cheerful looks and firm steps into the middle of the amphitheatre, where men with swords fell on them and dispatched them. The executioner who was to kill Perpetua was a youth, and was so nervous that he stabbed her in a place where the hurt was not deadly; but she herself took hold of his sword, and showed him where to give her the death-wound.[1]

MY LIFE WITH GOD EXERCISE

This story has become a classic among accounts about Christian martyrs. In contemporary times we have become familiar with these kind of scenarios in movies like *The Robe, Quo Vadis,* and *End of the Spear,* as well as classic books such as *Foxe's Book of Martyrs.* In spite of these accounts, most of us feel far removed from Christians' martyrdom. It is certainly easy to feel that way if we live in the West, where Christianity is the dominant religious tradition, but Christians around the world are still persecuted for their beliefs today in countries where the government is antagonistic toward Christianity or religion in general, such as China, North Korea, and parts of the Middle East. Do a Web search for contemporary Christian persecution or look up the topic at your local library. Some Web sites you might find helpful are International Christian Concern (www.persecution.org), Voice of the Martyrs (www.persecution.com), Christian Freedom International (www.christianfreedom.org), and Tears of the Oppressed (www.human-rights-and-christian-persecution.org). Then use the information on one of these Web sites or from your library search to write a letter asking for the release of a Christian jailed solely on the basis of faith, or write a letter of encouragement to the prisoner. If you do not feel free to write a letter, then put the persecution of Christians worldwide at the top of your prayer list.

Then take some time to shift your focus from the international to the national or local. It is clear that what is described on these Web sites is persecution—being unable to practice one's faith for fear of imprisonment or even death. But there are also subtler forms of persecution. *Webster's* defines the word *persecute* as "to harass in a manner designed to injure, grieve, or afflict; *specif.* to cause to suffer because of belief," and *persecution* as "the act or practice of persecuting esp. those who differ in origin, religion, or social outlook." Do you think that religious people in your country or community experience persecution? If so, how? Is it persecution when someone is sued for displaying a religious symbol or is not allowed to recite a prayer in a public ceremony? What about when Christians are called names, such as "Bible bashers"? Is the system of separation of church and state and the policies that derive from it persecution? Or is it only persecution when someone's life or family is threatened? What about within Christian churches themselves? Are there groups within your church or denomination that are experiencing persecution for different interpretations of the Bible? What religious traditions other than Christianity might be persecuted in our culture? What is your role as a Christian when you see those who practice other religious traditions being persecuted?

REFLECTING ON MY LIFE WITH GOD
Allow each member a few moments to answer this question.

What did you learn about contemporary religious persecution? What insights did you have about Christian persecution in your country, community, or church?

▶ SCRIPTURE READING: ACTS 6:8–15; 7:51–8:4

After everyone has had a chance to respond to the question, ask a member to read this passage from Scripture.

Stephen, full of grace and power, did great wonders and signs among the people. Then some of those who belonged to the synagogue of the Freedmen (as it was called), Cyrenians, Alexandrians, and others of those from Cilicia and Asia, stood up and argued with Stephen. But they could not withstand the wisdom and the Spirit with which he spoke. Then they secretly instigated some men to say, "We have heard him speak blasphemous words against Moses and God." They stirred up the people as well as the elders and the scribes; then they suddenly confronted him, seized him, and brought him before the council. They set up false witnesses who said, "This man never stops saying things against this holy place and the law; for we have heard him say that this Jesus of Nazareth will destroy this place and will change the customs that Moses handed on to us." And all who sat in the council looked intently at him, and they saw that his face was like the face of an angel. . . .

[Stephen said] "You stiff-necked people, uncircumcised in heart and ears, you are forever opposing the Holy Spirit, just as your ancestors used to do. Which of the prophets did your ancestors not persecute? They killed those who foretold the coming of the Righteous One, and now you have become his betrayers and murderers. You are the ones that received the law as ordained by angels, and yet you have not kept it."

When they heard these things, they became enraged and ground their teeth at Stephen. But filled with the Holy Spirit, he gazed into heaven and saw the glory of God and Jesus standing at the right hand of God. "Look," he said, "I see the heavens opened and the Son of Man standing at the right hand of God!" But they covered their ears, and with a loud shout all rushed together against him. Then they dragged him out of the city and began to stone him; and the witnesses laid their coats at the feet of a young man named Saul. When they were stoning Stephen, he prayed, "Lord Jesus, receive my spirit." Then he knelt down and cried out in a loud voice, "Lord, do not hold this sin against them." When he had said this, he died. And Saul approved of their killing him.

That day a severe persecution began against the church in Jerusalem, and all except the apostles were scattered throughout the countryside of Judea and Samaria. Devout men buried Stephen and made loud lamentation over him. But Saul was ravaging the church by entering house after house; dragging off both men and women, he committed them to prison.

Now those who were scattered went from place to place, proclaiming the word.

Why do you think the men at the synagogue and then those at the council reacted so violently to Stephen's actions and message?

REFLECTION QUESTION
Allow each person a few moments to respond to this question.

▶▶ GETTING THE PICTURE

Stephen was a Hellenist and one of the disciples chosen to serve food to widows. As we learned in chapter 6, Hellenists were Greek-speaking Jews who were born in the diaspora or who had converted to Judaism. The stoning of Stephen is the first of three consecutive events Luke highlights that take the gospel beyond the borders of its Jewish birth. The other two are Philip's preaching in Samaria and subsequent baptism of

◁ After a brief discussion, choose one person to read this section.

the Ethiopian eunuch and the conversion of Saul, who begins his ministry by preaching in Damascus.

The first time we met Stephen, Luke described him as being "a man full of faith and the Holy Spirit" (Acts 6:5). In the Scripture Reading, he is described as being "full of grace and power" and doing "great wonders and signs among the people." But he encountered opposition from the synagogue of the Freedmen. Apparently there were synagogues, such as this one in Jerusalem, where Jews from various geographic areas worshiped together. Most likely the common denominator for this particular synagogue was fluency in Greek, since that culture had spread throughout the Mediterranean world with the military campaigns of Alexander the Great in the fourth century BC. When the members of this synagogue "could not withstand the wisdom and the Spirit with which [Stephen] spoke" (v 10), they bring him before the council (v 12).

In Stephen's appearance before the Sanhedrin, the false witnesses accuse him of saying "Jesus of Nazareth will destroy this place and will change the customs that Moses handed on to us" (v 14). In first-century Judaism, the temple and Mosaic law were sacrosanct. The Herodian temple, like the magnificent first temple built by Solomon and the second temple built after the exile, was the seat of the religious leaders' positions and power. If it were to be destroyed again, their positions would disappear, and Jewish religious practice would be thrown into chaos. In answer to the high priest's question, "Are these things so?" (7:1), Stephen launches into a spirited defense by recounting the experiences of three people from their common religious heritage—Abraham, Joseph, and Moses, each of whom at least one time in his life was told to leave—ending with the example of the tabernacle in the wilderness as the ideal place to worship God, though "the Most High does not dwell in houses made with human hands" (v 48). This statement was probably interpreted by the council members as an attack on the temple, the seat of their power and influence.

In conclusion, Stephen uses several words to describe his questioners—stiff-necked, uncircumcised, and opposing—and states that they had betrayed and murdered the Righteous One just as their ancestors had killed the prophets who had predicted his coming. Calling them stiff-necked, the term God had used to describe the Israelites when they worshiped the golden calf while Moses was receiving the Ten Commandments on Mount Sinai (Exod 32:9; 33:3, 5; 34:9), implies that they are too proud to yield to God's yoke in obedience. To say the council members were uncircumcised of heart and ears is to say that they are

God's people in outward sign and name only, and recalls God's judgment against the apostates among the Israelites (Lev 26:41; Deut 10:16; Jer 4:4; 9:26). Telling the council members they are opposed to the Holy Spirit is accusing them of opposition to God. At the end, Stephen, the Hellenist, tells the council members that they are the ones who have changed the customs, not him.

Predictably, the council members become enraged, and Stephen's statement that he was able to see into heaven angers them further because they interpret it as blasphemy. If Stephen had not claimed to have seen into heaven, the Sanhedrin could have condemned him as an apostate and given him thirty-nine lashes. But in their eyes his openly blasphemous statement demands the death penalty. The phrase "dragged him out of the city" implies that they threw Stephen off one of the cliffs on which Jerusalem is built. When the fall does not kill him, they take their coats off and throw stones as heavy as they can lift down onto him.[2]

▶▶▶ GOING DEEPER

A remarkable aspect of this passage is Stephen's calmness and peace. His countenance is like that of an angel. According to the text, there was no such peace and assurance in the countenances of those on the council. It is clear that Stephen was filled with the Holy Spirit, which enabled him to speak truth to power. The Holy Spirit, and its assurance that Jesus Christ is with us always, enabled him and enables us not to fear even death. Now as then, the Holy Spirit gives us power to work for Jesus Christ and his kingdom regardless of the circumstances and the obstacles that we face. Without the Holy Spirit the apostles would have just been a band of no-name followers of a man who they claimed had risen from the dead. With the Holy Spirit they had the power and courage to follow Christ wherever he led, in whatever circumstances they faced. So it is for us.

Have another member read this section.

If we proclaim the gospel, we must expect opposition. Stephen's speech makes this clear: "Which of the prophets did your ancestors not persecute?" Throughout the history of the Jewish people, many of those who spoke God's word were subject to hard times and disbelief from those around them. The apostles had twice been brought up on charges before the council, but Stephen's appearance is the first time an ordinary disciple had been accused of attacking Israel's customs and traditions. Today we ordinary disciples, even those of us who live in countries where Christianity is the majority religious tradition and who are surrounded by Christian brothers and sisters, can expect to face challenges, mistrust, and ridicule, even from those within the Church, if we truly follow the path of Christ. This may take the form of being viewed as a "Bible-thumper" by those in our family or workplace; it might mean open hostility and distrust from those who have chosen to follow people or things other than Christ. For Stephen and countless others throughout the centuries, it has meant death. With the help of the Holy Spirit, we will have the strength to continue being disciples of Jesus Christ in spite of the opposition we face.

Finally, we have to be careful that we are promoting God's agenda, not our own. At times we forget that the conflict between Stephen and the council concerned two parties who both felt they were representing God. We know that the people who questioned Stephen had an agenda: to protect the primacy of the temple and the Mosaic law. But we have to remember that for them this was God's will. The Mosaic law and worship at the temple had been the way the Jewish people experienced God for centuries. These leaders had spent their lives studying and interpreting the law and worshiping at the temple, and they were not open to being led in a new direction. Stephen argued that following Jesus was totally different from Judaism and thus could not be included under Judaism's umbrella. The Jewish leaders could not see this radical message as coming from God. While their zeal for God was certainly appropriate, the Jewish leaders were unjustified in responding to the contrarian message of the early Christians with persecution through imprisonment and violence. In contrast, in whatever we attempt for the kingdom of God, especially when in disagreement with others, we should approach our efforts with prayer and humility, always seeking the guidance and wisdom of the Holy Spirit. We should aim to err on the side of grace and mercy. "My concern is not whether God is on our side; my greatest concern is to be on God's side, for God is always right," said Abraham Lincoln.

REFLECTION QUESTION
Allow each person a few moments to respond.

What opposition or persecution have you faced, if any, because of your Christian faith?

▶▶▶▶ POINTING TO GOD

🕊 Choose one member to read this section.

One prominent modern example of someone who felt called by his Christian faith to follow a certain path in the world and was then persecuted for it is the Reverend Martin Luther King Jr. Born in 1929, King emerged as a leader early in his educational career, when he was elected president of his predominantly white class at Crozer Theological Seminary. He went on to receive a doctorate from Boston University in 1955, becoming pastor of the Dexter Avenue Baptist Church in Montgomery, Alabama, and serving on the executive committee of the National Association for the Advancement of Colored People. Late in 1955, he gained national notice for leading the famous 382-day Montgomery bus boycott to protest bus segregation laws, which ended in December 1956, when the U.S. Supreme Court declared such laws unconstitutional. Shortly thereafter, King was elected president of the Southern Christian Leadership Conference. In this capacity, he spoke all over the country and both led and joined many peaceful protests against racial inequality, receiving the Nobel Peace Prize for his work. At thirty-five, King was the youngest man ever to receive the honor. Just a few years later, Dr. King was assassinated in 1968 in Memphis, Tennessee, on the eve of a march in sympathy with striking garbage workers.

In arguing for equal rights for people of all races and colors, he faced serious opposition: his house was bombed; he was harassed by police, arrested once for driving 30 mph in a 25 mph zone, and repeatedly jailed for his participation in protest marches; and he received numerous death threats. In the last months of his life, there was reportedly a $50,000 bounty on his head.[3]

With hindsight, King is now remembered as a political hero and a martyr for the Church, but while he was speaking and leading marches many prominent church leaders strongly resisted his ideas and his tactics of nonviolent direct action. On April 19, 1963, after being arrested for leading a protest, King famously addressed a group of white clergymen who were critical of his tactics of direct action in his "Letter from Birmingham Jail." In it he made it clear that his actions were influenced by the gospel, writing, "I am in Birmingham because injustice is here. Just as the prophets of the eighth century B.C. left their villages and carried their 'thus saith the Lord' far beyond the boundaries of their home towns, and just as the Apostle Paul left his village of Tarsus and carried the gospel of Jesus Christ to the far corners of the Greco-Roman world, so am I compelled to carry the gospel of freedom beyond my own home town. Like Paul, I must constantly respond to the Macedonian call for aid."[4] Further, he stated that his tactics were biblical and in the Christian tradition: "There is nothing new about this kind of civil disobedience. It was evidenced sublimely in the refusal of Shadrach, Meshach and Abednego to obey the laws of Nebuchadnezzar, on the ground that a higher moral law was at stake. It was practiced superbly by the early Christians, who were willing to face hungry lions and the excruciating pain of chopping blocks rather than submit to certain unjust laws of the Roman Empire."[5] And, finally, he turned the white pastors' criticism on its head by pointing it out for what it was, a sanctioning of the status quo: "So often the contemporary church is a weak, ineffectual voice with an uncertain sound. So often it is an archdefender of the status quo. Far from being disturbed by the presence of the church, the power structure of the average community is consoled by the church's silent—and often even vocal—sanction of things as they are."[6] (A large portion of this letter is reprinted as the Devotional Reading for chapter 11. You may wish to read it now.)

▶▶▶▶▶ GOING FORWARD

Have another person read this section.

As we become familiar with the powerful words of King's "Letter from Birmingham Jail," we must wonder if we too, like the Jewish council, have perhaps been guilty of silently or vocally sanctioning the status quo and, as such, unintentionally persecuting others. The members of the Sanhedrin were protecting the worship of God as they had always known it. The white pastors who wrote King also were sanctioning the status quo. Whether or not they thought King was proclaiming the gospel with his words and actions, they urged him to wait, to quiet down, to obey the law, to honor the ways things had always been. With hindsight, we can see that both the council and the white pastors were turning a blind eye to the stirrings of God.

Those who refuse to stop proclaiming the gospel with their words and actions will likely face opposition. We know that the message of the gospel is an audacious one and that those who choose not to listen to it will not be supportive of those who proclaim it. Jesus never promised us that proclaiming the gospel would keep us safe here on earth; indeed, his death showed us just the opposite. Those of us who live in countries where being a Christian is relatively safe have to guard against complacency. We must listen for the guidance of the Holy Spirit, even when it leads us against the status quo, against the way things have always been. And in so doing, we often will place ourselves in the path of persecution.

REFLECTION QUESTION
Again, allow each member a few moments to answer this question.

What are some other examples in Christian history or your own experience of church leaders rejecting God's messengers because the leaders were too comfortable with the status quo?

LIVING THE MISSION

This concludes our look at experiencing persecution. In the next chapter we will turn our attention to another avenue of living the mission—converting the mind.

CLOSING PRAYER

I will extol you, my God and King,
    and bless your name forever and ever.
Every day I will bless you,
    and praise your name forever and ever.
Great is the LORD, and greatly to be praised;
    his greatness is unsearchable.

One generation shall laud your works to another,
    and shall declare your mighty acts.
On the glorious splendor of your majesty,
    and on your wondrous works, I will meditate.
The might of your awesome deeds shall be proclaimed,
    And I will declare your greatness. (PS 145:1–6)

◁ After everyone has had a chance to respond, the leader reads this paragraph.

◁ **Allow some time for members to encourage one another to read the Devotional and Scripture Readings and do the exercise in the following chapter before the next meeting.** Then invite the members to be silent for a few moments before leading them in reading the Closing Prayer aloud together.

◁ At the end of the Closing Prayer, the leader asks for a volunteer to lead the next meeting.

TAKING IT FURTHER

ADDITIONAL EXERCISE

Find a copy of Martin Luther King Jr.'s "Letter from Birmingham Jail" on the Internet or at your local library and read it in its entirety. Try to see the issues he is writing about from the viewpoint of the pastors to whom he is responding, as well as from King's perspective. How do you think they came to their conclusions? What do you think your reaction would be to receiving a response such as King's?

ADDITIONAL RESOURCES

Eliot, Elisabeth. *Shadow of the Almighty*. San Francisco: HarperSanFrancisco, 1989.

Foxe, John, and William Byron Forbush. *Foxe's Book of Martyrs*. Grand Rapids, MI: Zondervan, 1978.

Quo Vadis. MGM, 1951.

The Robe. Twentieth Century Fox, 1953.

Saint, Steve. *End of the Spear*. Carol Stream, IL: Salt River, 2005. Also a major motion picture from Twentieth Century Fox, 2005.

How might your faith and the way you practice it differ from the faith practiced by those who live under the fear of persecution or even death for their beliefs?

Most of us will never face persecution like that faced by Stephen, Perpetua, or Martin Luther King Jr. What are the distinctive dangers and challenges faced by a church such as ours in the West and its members, in a place where Christianity is the dominant religious tradition and most people are at least nominally Christian?

How can we as Christians remain open to the call of the Holy Spirit, even when it goes against the will of God as we previously understood it?

CONVERTING THE MIND

9

DEVOTIONAL READING

ALISTER MCGRATH, "God as My Guide"

Spiritually, God is the oxygen of my existence; I would find it very difficult to thrive without a belief in God.... I haven't always seen things this way. When I was growing up in Belfast, Northern Ireland, during the 1960s, I came to the view that God was an infantile illusion, suitable for the elderly, the intellectually feeble, and the fraudulently religious. I admit this was a rather arrogant view, and one that I now find somewhat embarrassing. My rather pathetic excuse for this intellectual haughtiness is that a lot of other people felt the same way back then. It was the received wisdom of the day that religion was on its way out, and that a glorious, godless dawn was just around the corner.

Part of the reasoning that led to my conclusion was based on the natural sciences. I had specialized in mathematics and science during high school, as preparation for going to Oxford University to study chemistry. While my primary motivations for studying the sciences were the insights they allowed into the wonderful world of nature, I also found them a convenient ally in my critique of religion. Atheism and the natural sciences seemed to be coupled together by the most rigorous bonds. And there things rested, until I arrived at Oxford in October 1971.

Chemistry proved to be intellectually exhilarating. As more and more of the complexities of the natural world seemed to fall into place, I found myself overwhelmed by an incandescent enthusiasm.... In the midst of this growing delight in the natural sciences, which exceeded anything I could have hoped for, I found myself rethinking my atheism. It is not easy for anyone to subject his core beliefs to criticism; my reason for doing so was the growing realization that things were not quite as straightforward as I had once thought.

It is helpful for everyone to read the Devotional and Scripture Readings and do the My Life with God Exercise before the meeting. Begin the meeting with silent prayer, then move directly to Reflecting on My Life with God below.

Atheism, I began to realize, rested on a less-than-satisfactory evidential basis. The arguments that had once seemed bold, decisive, and conclusive increasingly turned out to be circular, tentative, and uncertain. The opportunity to talk with Christians about their faith revealed to me that I understood relatively little about their religion, which I had come to know chiefly through not-always-accurate descriptions by its leading critics, including British logician Bertrand Russell and German social philosopher Karl Marx. I also began to realize that my assumption of the automatic and inexorable link between the natural sciences and atheism was rather naïve and uninformed. One of the most important things I had to sort out, after my conversion to Christianity, was the systematic uncoupling of this bond. Instead, I would see the natural sciences from a Christian perspective—and I would try to understand why others did not share this perspective. . . .

Belief in God, [Richard Dawkins] argues, is like believing in Santa Claus or the tooth fairy: It cannot be sustained when we grow up and learn the realities of the scientific method . . . Yet . . . [t]he scientific method simply does not allow us to adjudicate the existence of God, and those who force it to do so (on either side of the debate) have pressed it beyond its acceptable limits. In one sense, both theism and atheism must be recognized as positions of faith, belief systems that go beyond the available scientific evidence. . . . Atheism is not the only conceivable worldview for a thinking person. Belief in God gives us reason to examine the universe more closely, and generates a matrix that both encourages and facilitates an engagement with the world.[1]

MY LIFE WITH GOD EXERCISE

Many of us can relate to Alister McGrath's journey from finding the claims of Christianity far-fetched to coming to a place where these claims became the center of a new worldview. To McGrath, God now "illuminates the great riddles and enigmas of life, including how and why it is that we can make sense of the universe at all."[2] For some, this understanding was our first important step in becoming a Christian. Others found coming to Christ a more emotional experience, led more by our hearts than by our minds. Many of us still struggle at times to reconcile our belief in God with our thoughts and understandings about the world around us. Whatever our experience, at one point or another in our faith journey we must explore our faith from an intellectual angle.

For this exercise, we would like you to try to trace the history of how you have intellectually perceived God over the course of your life. Did you have any initial misconceptions about God—perhaps confusing him with an authority figure in your life or even viewing him as akin to Santa Claus or the Tooth Fairy? How has your understanding of God progressed over time? It might help to divide your life into time periods, say every ten years, and reflect on them separately during your regular time alone with God. Ask yourself: Are there any biblical teachings about God that I have trouble believing intellectually? For example, do I find it intellectually hard to believe that Jesus Christ is God? If I do, what are the reasons? If not, did I come to this place of understanding gradually or all at once? If you do not have a difficult time believing that Jesus Christ is God, give those reasons. Feel free to share your doubts or certainties about the divinity of Jesus Christ or other Christian teaching with another person whom you know is reflecting on similar topics.

What did you learn about your intellectual understanding of Jesus?

REFLECTING ON MY LIFE WITH GOD
Allow each member a few moments to answer this question.

▶ SCRIPTURE READING: ACTS 9:1–20

✍ After everyone has had a chance to respond to the question, ask a member to read this passage from Scripture.

Meanwhile Saul, still breathing threats and murder against the disciples of the Lord, went to the high priest and asked him for letters to the synagogues at Damascus, so that if he found any who belonged to the Way, men or women, he might bring them bound to Jerusalem. Now as he was going along and approaching Damascus, suddenly a light from heaven flashed around him. He fell to the ground and heard a voice saying to him, "Saul, Saul, why do you persecute me?" He asked, "Who are you, Lord?" The reply came, "I am Jesus, whom you are persecuting. But get up and enter the city, and you will be told what you are to do." The men who were traveling with him stood speechless because they heard the voice but saw no one. Saul got up from the ground, and though his eyes were open, he could see nothing; so they led him by the hand and brought him into Damascus. For three days he was without sight, and neither ate nor drank.

Now there was a disciple in Damascus named Ananias. The Lord said to him in a vision, "Ananias." He answered, "Here I am, Lord." The Lord said to him, "Get up and go to the street called Straight, and at the house of Judas look for a man of Tarsus named Saul. At this moment he is praying, and he has seen in a vision a man named Ananias come in and lay his hands on him so that he might regain his sight." But Ananias answered, "Lord, I have heard from many about this man, how much evil he has done to your saints in Jerusalem; and here he has authority from the chief priests to bind all who invoke your name." But the Lord said to him, "Go, for he is an instrument whom I have chosen to bring my name before Gentiles and kings and before the people of Israel; I myself will show him how much he must suffer for the sake of my name." So Ananias went and entered the house. He laid his hands on Saul and said, "Brother Saul, the Lord Jesus, who appeared to you on your way here, has sent me so that you may regain your sight and be filled with the Holy Spirit." And immediately something like scales fell from his eyes, and his sight was restored. Then he got up and was baptized, and after taking some food, he regained his strength.

For several days he was with the disciples in Damascus, and immediately he began to proclaim Jesus in the synagogues, saying, "He is the Son of God."

REFLECTION QUESTION
Allow each person a few moments to respond to this question.

Which elements of Saul's famous conversion experience correspond to your own? Which are different?

➤➤ GETTING THE PICTURE

After a brief discussion, choose one person to read this section.

We first met Saul in Acts as he stood over the clothes of his fellow council members while they were stoning Stephen to death. In his own words, Saul was "circumcised on the eighth day, a member of the people of Israel, of the tribe of Benjamin, a Hebrew born of Hebrews; as to the law, a Pharisee; as to zeal, a persecutor of the church; as to righteousness under the law, blameless" (Phil 3:5–6). We know he had been well educated in the renowned schools of the Roman city of Tarsus and had learned the philosophy and poetry of the Greeks. He had then learned theology and Jewish law at Jerusalem, taught by the eminent Pharisee scholar Gamaliel (Acts 22:3). He was a man of impeccable ancestry, education, motivation, and morality.

After the stoning of Stephen, Saul participated in "a severe persecution . . . against the church in Jerusalem, and all except the apostles were scattered throughout the countryside of Judea and Samaria" (Acts 8:1b). To escape Saul's fury, Philip went to the city of Samaria, where he proclaimed the Messiah to the people and performed miracles in their midst. Many were baptized, and Peter and John joined Philip in Samaria to pray for them. In the meantime, Saul secures letters of introduction addressed to the synagogues in Damascus, a town 134 miles from Jerusalem with a large number of prosperous Jews. Since Saul is authorized to bring the Jews from Damascus back to Jersualem, we can infer that his plans were approved by the political ruler of Judea, most likely the Jewish king Herod Agrippa (see Acts 12:19b–23). And since the prisoners were to be "bound"—in chains or worse—the men described as traveling with him were probably temple police to help arrest and transport them.

The light that surrounds Saul on his trip to Damascus is the second record of a visible manifestation of God's presence in the book of Acts, the first being on the day of Pentecost recorded in Acts 2. The key question asked of Saul was, "Why do you persecute me?" Saul has no response. Instead he asks, from the position where he had fallen on the ground, "Who are you, Lord?" Using the word *Lord,* a title of respect that recognizes the addressee's power and authority, demonstrates Paul's reverence for the one he was addressing even though he did not yet know who was responsible for the bright light and the voice calling his name. His immediate reaction makes us wonder if Saul had doubts on any level about what he was doing. Jesus's response, "I am Jesus, whom you are persecuting," certainly would have thrown an already doubting man into turmoil about his actions. When Jesus tells Saul to go on into Damascus, where he would get further instructions, he obeys.

Meanwhile, Jesus appears also to Ananias, telling him to go to Saul. It is apparent from Ananias's reaction to his vision that he knows of and fears not only Saul but also the place or the people with whom he is staying. We can surmise that Saul was staying in a non-Christian household, most likely with a friend or acquaintance, possibly even the place where he had arranged to stay while he was rounding up Christians to take back to Jerusalem. So Ananias's reluctance is perfectly understandable. However, Ananias overcomes his reticence, obeys God, and goes directly to Straight Street, where he ministers to Saul.

▶▶▶ GOING DEEPER

Saul's 180-degree change from "breathing threats and murder against the disciples of the Lord" to becoming a follower himself is certainly a dramatic example of a conversion of the mind. He who had understood the Christians to be so dangerous that he took it upon himself to persecute

Have another member read this section.

them became arguably the early Church's most vocal advocate. The most obvious spiritual formation principle that we can glean from Saul's conversion is that we should be careful about appointing ourselves chief investigator and prosecutor of those people we believe are deviating from our understanding of the kingdom. Given Saul's background and training, it was natural for him to feel that he understood God and the law, and that everyone who saw things differently was suspect. This is a hazard we all face as we work in the kingdom. For example, if we have been called to work with the poor, we are tempted to look down on all those who do not do the same. Or we think that everyone except the people in our particular fellowship or denomination has a skewed understanding of Scripture. We must always remember that we are to serve the Lord as he calls us, and that it is his prerogative to call others to serve and understand the Scripture as he wills, not as we will.

Saul's decision to follow Christ was heralded by a period of fasting and prayer, both of which are marks of intense spiritual endeavor. We know that Saul was an educated man; we can imagine that he was furiously working out the implications of belief in Jesus. His three days of fasting and prayer surely helped to clarify and focus his thinking about the incredible situation he faced. On top of everything, the encounter had blinded him, so that he had to depend on the other men to lead him to their destination. Saul reacted to this frightening situation not by turning from God or railing at him for the unfairness of it, but by turning to God in prayer and fasting. He had enough humility to know that the situation was beyond his control, which was the first step to letting God be in charge of his life.

When we come to a place where we are ready to believe, God will prepare a person to minister to us. God prepared Ananias to go to Saul as he was preparing Saul's heart for ministry to the Gentiles. Two events were happening simultaneously in Saul's conversion: Ananias's heart was softening toward the man who was doing the persecuting, and Saul's heart was softening toward the people he was persecuting. When both of them were ready, Ananias went to Saul, laid his hands on him, and greeted him as "Brother Saul." We too need the fellowship of other Christians in order to receive the blessings of God. Saul regained his sight through the action of Ananias. Think what might have happened if Saul had been so full of pride that he rejected Ananias's ministry. But instead, when Saul found himself in a situation where he knew he needed help, in spite of his pure ancestry, his extensive education, and his self-righteousness, he humbled himself and received the prayers of a man whom he had come to Damascus to arrest. As a result he found fellowship, regained his eyesight, received the Holy Spirit, and was baptized at the hands of Ananias. Neither can we do ministry by ourselves.

What person or group of people did God prepare to help you in your initial conversion or at a crucial point in your discipleship?

REFLECTION QUESTION
Allow each person a few moments to respond.

>>>> POINTING TO GOD

Like Saul, nineteenth-century Russian writer Leo Tolstoy was born to a prominent family and sent to a respected university, although he grew disillusioned with formal education and never earned his degree. The Russia of his day was marked by huge inequities between rich and poor, with the vast majority of the population serving the landowners as serfs and possessing very little education or legal rights. Tolstoy was moved by the plight of the serfs who worked his family's land, and as he recorded in his novel *A Landowner's Morning,* he attempted to improve their lot in life by abolishing beatings as a form of punishment, establishing a school for them, and giving them lectures on self-improvement. Predictably the laborers reacted with suspicion, and Tolstoy quickly gave up, leaving the country life for that of the city. His concern for social inequities, however, would remain with him throughout his life.

Choose one member to read this section.

A few years later, he joined the Russian army, where he was again horrified by the plight of the involuntarily enlisted peasants who, until reforms were made in 1863, were required to serve twenty-five years. Discipline was incredibly harsh, and perhaps worst of all, much of their military careers were spent fighting other peasants, mainly rural laborers who had risen up to demand more legal rights and basic provisions. When Tolstoy returned to his family estate, he tried again to make life better for the peasants who lived and worked there. He began a school and overcame the resistance he had experienced in his earlier efforts by teaching while dressed in peasant clothing to establish some common ground with his students. He became a great champion of peasants, incurring the wrath of fellow landowners and the government alike. Meanwhile, he was putting his thoughts about war and social justice into his epic *War and Peace* and then his story about a woman tragically disappointed by romantic love, *Anna Karenina.*

After completing these two novels, however, Tolstoy plunged into a depression. The philosophy he espoused in both books—a moral he

Converting the Mind

summed up later as "One should live so as to have the best for oneself and one's family"—no longer seemed valid to him.[3] Although he had been baptized and brought up in the Russian Orthodox Church, Tolstoy as a young man "drew the conclusion that it is necessary to learn the Catechism and it is necessary to go to church, but that one need not take it all too seriously."[4] At this point, however, inspired by the faith of the peasants, with whom he was spending more and more time, Tolstoy found new meaning in the teachings of Christ, particularly Jesus's statement in the Sermon on the Mount, "Do not resist an evildoer. But if anyone strikes you on the right cheek, turn the other also" (Matt 5:39), which advocated nonresistance in the face of violence. This doctrine fit with his disillusionment over the brutality he had seen in the army. Tolstoy famously said, "Christianity, with its doctrine of humility, of forgiveness, of love, is incompatible with the State, with its haughtiness, its violence, its punishment, its wars." His intellectual acquiescence to Jesus's teachings sparked a conversion and also inspired him to go even further with his commitment to social justice and a life of simplicity. He renounced his property rights, giving much of his property away to family members, and dressed only in peasant clothing. The rest of his writings bore the marks of his faith, including *A Confession,* in which he details his conversion, and the famous short story "The Death of Ivan Ilyich," in which he describes a man who undergoes a spiritual conversion on his deathbed.

▶▶▶▶▶ GOING FORWARD

⚐ Have another person read this section.

We may read of Saul's and Leo Tolstoy's conversions with interest but without seeing any real connection to our own spiritual formation. After all, if we are already Christians, we may feel our conversion is a done deal. We have accepted Christ and that is that. But maybe it is not so easy. Maybe we have accepted Christ with our heart but not with our mind; perhaps we cannot quite bring ourselves to believe that Jesus is God. Or perhaps we can intellectually accept this, but we have not yet committed with our whole hearts to becoming a disciple of Jesus Christ, something we will talk about more in the next chapter. Martin Luther famously said that there are three conversions: the conversion of the mind, the conversion of the heart, and the conversion of the purse. Committing to Jesus Christ involves our whole self (and our resources as well) and sometimes even we are unaware that we have held some-

LIVING THE MISSION

thing back. Perhaps it is better to view our commitment not as a one-time deal, but as a process, a journey, of turning ever closer to God, learning more about him and his ways, and striving to become ever more like Jesus.

Have you experienced conversions of the heart, mind, and purse? Did they happen separately or all at once? Please explain.

REFLECTION QUESTION
Again, allow each member a few moments to answer this question.

This concludes our look at converting the mind. In the next chapter we will turn our attention to another avenue of living the mission—converting the heart.

✍ After everyone has had a chance to respond, the leader reads this paragraph.

✍ **Allow some time for members to encourage one another to read the Devotional and Scripture Readings and do the exercise in the following chapter before the next meeting.** Then invite the members to be silent for a few moments before leading them in reading the Closing Prayer aloud together.

✍ At the end of the Closing Prayer, the leader asks for a volunteer to lead the next meeting.

CLOSING PRAYER

I will extol you, my God and King,
    and bless your name forever and ever.
Every day I will bless you,
    and praise your name forever and ever.
Great is the LORD, and greatly to be praised;
    his greatness is unsearchable.

One generation shall laud your works to another,
    and shall declare your mighty acts.
On the glorious splendor of your majesty,
    and on your wondrous works, I will meditate.
The might of your awesome deeds shall be proclaimed,
    And I will declare your greatness. (PS 145:1–6)

TAKING IT FURTHER

In your small group or on your own, read Tolstoy's *The Death of Ivan Ilyich*. What parallels do you see with what you know of Tolstoy's story? What insights did you gain about the process of coming to Christ?

ADDITIONAL EXERCISE

McDowell, Josh. *Evidence That Demands a Verdict*. Rev. ed. San Bernardino, CA: Here's Life, 1979.
Phillips, J. B. *Your God Is Too Small*. New York: Macmillan, 1961.
Tolstoy, Leo. *A Confession and Other Religious Writings*. Translated by Jane Kentish. London: Penguin, 1988.

ADDITIONAL RESOURCES

Do you know of anyone who has experienced a conversion of the mind and not the heart or vice versa? Explain. What might you do to help that person move forward?

What significance do you see in the fact that Saul was struck blind for three days following his experience on the road to Damascus?

Did the disciplines of fasting and prayer play any role in your initial decision to follow Christ? If so, how?

CONVERTING THE HEART

10

KEY SCRIPTURE: Acts 10:1–17, 19–23a, 24b–36, 44–48

DEVOTIONAL READING

ELLEN G. WHITE, "Genuine Conversion"

Conversion is a change of heart, a turning from unrighteousness to righteousness. Relying upon the merits of Christ, exercising true faith in him, the repentant sinner receives pardon for sin. As he ceases to do evil, and learns to do well, he grows in grace and in the knowledge of God. He sees that in order to follow Jesus he must separate from the world, and, after counting the cost, he looks upon all as loss if he may but win Christ. He enlists in his army, and bravely and cheerfully engages in the warfare, fighting against natural inclinations and selfish desires, and bringing the will into subjection to the will of Christ. Daily he seeks the Lord for grace, and he is strengthened and helped. Self once reigned in his heart, and worldly pleasure was his delight. Now self is dethroned, and God reigns supreme. His life reveals the fruit of righteousness. The sins he once loved he now hates. Firmly and resolutely he follows in the path of holiness. This is genuine conversion.

In the lives of many of those whose names are on the church books there has been no genuine change. The truth has been kept in the outer court. There has been no genuine conversion, no positive work of grace done in the heart. Their desire to do God's will is based upon their own inclination, not upon the deep conviction of the Holy Spirit. Their conduct is not brought into harmony with the law of God. They profess to accept Christ as their Saviour, but they do not believe that he will give them power to overcome their sins. They have not a personal acquaintance with a living Saviour, and their characters reveal many blemishes.

Many a one who looks at himself in the divine mirror, and is convinced that his life is not what it ought to be, fails to make the needed change. He goes his way, and forgets his defects. He may profess to be

It is helpful for everyone to read the Devotional and Scripture Readings and do the My Life with God Exercise before the meeting. Begin the meeting with silent prayer, then move directly to Reflecting on My Life with God below.

a follower of Christ, but what does this avail if his character has undergone no change, if the Holy Spirit has not wrought upon his heart? The work done has been superficial. Self is retained in his life. He is not a partaker of the divine nature. He may talk of God and pray to God, but his life reveals that he is working against God.

Let us not forget that in his conversion and sanctification, man must cooperate with God. "Work out your own salvation with fear and trembling," the Word declares; "for it is God which worketh in you both to will and to do of his good pleasure." Man can not transform himself by the exercise of his will. He possesses no power by which this change may be effected. The renewing energy must come from God. The change can be made only by the Holy Spirit. He who would be saved, high or low, rich or poor, must submit to the working of this power.

As the leaven, when mingled with the meal, works from within outward, so it is by the renewing of the heart that the grace of God works to transform the life. No mere external change is sufficient to bring us into harmony with God. There are many who try to reform by correcting this bad habit or that bad habit, and they hope in this way to become Christians, but they are beginning in the wrong place. Our first work is with the heart.[1]

MY LIFE WITH GOD EXERCISE

Ellen White writes, "Let us not forget that in his conversion and sanctification,* man must cooperate with God.... The renewing energy must come from God. The change can be made only by the Holy Spirit." This is true as far as it goes, but she fails to offer any specific way that the energy and power of the Holy Spirit can be released in us to bring our conduct into harmony with the law of God, other than through a conversion of the heart. Important as it is, many of us know that the conversion of the heart does not automatically translate overnight into a sinless life. This is one of the hardest issues that followers of Christ face: how to overcome bad habits that cause us to hurt other people and ourselves—what the Bible calls sin, which is still with us after we are born from above and empowered by the Holy Spirit. Sometimes a habit is immediately eradicated upon conversion; many of us know people who have experienced this liberation. Other habits seem to hang on and on until we despair whether their hold on us will ever be broken.

* The state of growing in divine grace as a result of Christian commitment after baptism or conversion.

In the Introduction to *Celebration of Discipline*, Richard Foster proposes a solution to the problem of Christians wanting to overcome bad habits but failing to do so. He concurs with Ellen White: "The needed change within us is God's work, not ours. The demand is for an inside job, and only God can work from the inside. We cannot attain or earn this righteousness of the kingdom of God; it is a grace that is given." He then offers a way we can open ourselves to God's work: "God has given us the Disciplines of the spiritual life as a means of receiving his grace. The Disciplines allow us to place ourselves before God so that he can transform us."[2]

Foster discusses twelve Disciplines of the Spirit in *Celebration of Discipline:* meditation, prayer, fasting, study, simplicity, solitude, submission, service, worship, guidance, confession, and celebration. Before reading the next chapter, engage in a Spiritual Discipline that you have never tried before. You might try one of the Inward Disciplines, for example, fasting—the voluntary denial of an otherwise normal function for the sake of intense spiritual activity. When thinking of fasting, most people picture abstaining from food. It can also include refraining from watching your favorite television show or working on your hobby or reading the newspaper, so as to spend the time in prayer or service. Or you could try an Outward Discipline, such as submission—the discipline that allows us to let go of the everlasting burden of always needing to get our own way. This entails submitting to the wishes of another person instead of demanding that a task be done our way. Or a Corporate Discipline, perhaps guidance—the experience of knowing in our lives an interactive friendship with God. Guidance not only implies seeking help from the Lord about decisions we face every day but suggests swallowing our pride and asking for help from another person or persons. We hope these examples help you with this exercise. Should you need further help in understanding the discipline you try, *Celebration of Discipline* is a good resource.

What discipline did you try? What was your experience?

REFLECTING ON MY LIFE WITH GOD
Allow each member a few moments to answer this question.

► **SCRIPTURE READING:** ACTS 10:1–17, 19–23A, 24B–36, 44–48

After everyone has had a chance to respond to the question, ask a member to read this passage from Scripture.

In Caesarea there was a man named Cornelius, a centurion of the Italian Cohort, as it was called. He was a devout man who feared God with all his household; he gave alms generously to the people and prayed constantly to God. One afternoon at about three o'clock he had a vision in which he clearly saw an angel of God coming in and saying to him;

"Cornelius." He stared at him in terror and said, "What is it, Lord?" He answered, "Your prayers and your alms have ascended as a memorial before God. Now send men to Joppa for a certain Simon who is called Peter; he is lodging with Simon, a tanner, whose house is by the seaside." When the angel who spoke to him had left, he called two of his slaves and a devout soldier from the ranks of those who served him, and after telling them everything, he sent them to Joppa.

About noon the next day, as they were on their journey and approaching the city, Peter went up on the roof to pray. He became hungry and wanted something to eat; and while it was being prepared, he fell into a trance. He saw the heaven opened and something like a large sheet coming down, being lowered to the ground by its four corners. In it were all kinds of four-footed creatures and reptiles and birds of the air. Then he heard a voice saying, "Get up, Peter; kill and eat." But Peter said, "By no means, Lord; for I have never eaten anything that is profane or unclean." The voice said to him again, a second time, "What God has made clean, you must not call profane." This happened three times, and the thing was suddenly taken up to heaven.

Now while Peter was greatly puzzled about what to make of the vision that he had seen, suddenly the men sent by Cornelius appeared.... While Peter was still thinking about the vision, the Spirit said to him, "Look, three men are searching for you. Now get up, go down, and go with them without hesitation; for I have sent them." So Peter went down to the men and said, "I am the one you are looking for; what is the reason for your coming?" They answered, "Cornelius, a centurion, an upright and God-fearing man, who is well spoken of by the whole Jewish nation, was directed by a holy angel to send for you to come to his house and to hear what you have to say." So Peter invited them in and gave them lodging.

The next day he got up and went with them.... Cornelius was expecting them and had called together his relatives and close friends. On Peter's arrival Cornelius met him, and falling at his feet, worshiped him. But Peter made him get up, saying, "Stand up; I am only a mortal." And as he talked with him, he went in and found that many had assembled; and he said to them, "You yourselves know that it is unlawful for a Jew to associate with or to visit a Gentile; but God has shown me that I should not call anyone profane or unclean. So when I was sent for, I came without objection. Now may I ask why you sent for me?"

Cornelius replied, "Four days ago at this very hour, at three o'clock, I was praying in my house when suddenly a man in dazzling clothes stood before me. He said, 'Cornelius, your prayer has been heard and your alms have been remembered before God. Send therefore to Joppa and ask for Simon, who is called Peter; he is staying in the home of Simon, a tanner, by the sea.' Therefore I sent for you immediately, and you have been kind enough to come. So now all of us are here in the presence of God to listen to all that the Lord has commanded you to say."

Then Peter began to speak to them, "I truly understand that God shows no partiality, but in every nation anyone who fears him and does what is right is acceptable to him. You know the message he sent to the people of Israel, preaching peace by Jesus Christ—he is Lord of all. . . . While Peter was still speaking, the Holy Spirit fell upon all who heard the word. The circumcised believers who had come with Peter were astounded that the gift of the Holy Spirit had been poured out even on the Gentiles, for they heard them speaking in tongues and extolling God. Then Peter said, "Can anyone withhold the water for baptizing these people who have received the Holy Spirit just as we have?" So he ordered them to be baptized in the name of Jesus Christ. Then they invited him to stay for several days.

What person or group might you not have expected the Holy Spirit to touch— in the past or in your current thinking?

REFLECTION QUESTION
Allow each person a few moments to respond to this question.

▶▶ GETTING THE PICTURE

Our Scripture Reading begins with a Roman centurion named Cornelius. Although Cornelius was a Gentile, he is described in the passage as "devout" and "God-fearing" (10:2, 22). His men referred to him as "well spoken of by the whole Jewish nation" (v 22). Most likely he and his household were "God-fearers," Gentiles who were associated with the local synagogue but were not circumcised Jewish converts and thus not part of God's covenant with Israel.[3] Although he was neither a Jew nor a disciple, Cornelius clearly knows enough of God to recognize the angel in his vision as being from God. He obeys the angel's instructions without hesitation.

After a brief discussion, choose one person to read this section.

Meanwhile, Peter is staying in Joppa, where he "went up on the roof to pray" (10:9) and then falls into a trance and has the vision of the sheetlike object filled with all kinds of mammals, reptiles, and birds. When the voice commands him to kill and eat, Peter answers automatically, "By no means, Lord; for I have never eaten anything that is profane or unclean." For Peter, this was a no-brainer. The Mosaic law he had followed all his life strictly forbade him to eat any animals that were classified as unclean, including pigs and certain birds, such as eagles and buzzards (Lev 11:13–14). Therefore it must have been quite a shock to him when the voice replies, "What God has made clean, you must not call profane" (v 15). Greatly puzzled, Peter is still pondering the meaning of the vision when Cornelius's messengers find him. Peter too responds immediately to the Spirit's leading, and not only goes down to greet them but invites them to stay in his host's home and sets out with them the next day for the long journey to Caesarea.

There Peter finds waiting for him not only Cornelius but all of Cornelius's relatives and close friends. We see that Peter has understood the meaning of his vision when he tells Cornelius that even though as a Jew he is not supposed to associate with Gentiles, God has instructed him that he should not call anyone unclean or profane. Cornelius emphasizes that they are all ready to hear what Peter has to say, and not surprisingly, when Peter tells them the good news of Jesus Christ, they are filled with the Holy Spirit.

▶▶▶ GOING DEEPER

✑ Have another member read this section.

In this Scripture Reading we have examples of both a heart that has already been converted, Peter's, and a heart that is prepared to be converted, Cornelius's. What do they have in common? A complete openness to God and a willingness to follow his leadings without hesitation. In Peter's case, it is difficult to overemphasize just how hard it must have been for him to accept the meaning of his vision of the animals. Yet he did. We must remember that even though the apostle Peter was the leader of the disciples in Jerusalem and had already faced opposition when he taught about Jesus, he was Jewish. His loyalties were with Judaism. The Mosaic law was all about divisions between sacred and profane, clean and unclean—distinctions that applied to people as well as to animals. It was no doubt very difficult for Peter to accept that the clear delineations he had understood and followed all his life were no longer valid. Even though Jesus's teachings and actions—for example, his conversation with the Samaritan woman in John 4—had paved the way for this revelation, on at least one occasion Peter's loyalty to Judaism had been reinforced when Jesus hesitated to heal a Canaanite woman's daughter with the statement, "I was sent only to the lost sheep of the house of Israel" (Matt 15:24). Though the woman's faith led to the healing of her daughter, this incident probably convinced Peter that belief in Jesus would be confined to Jews. So Peter had a great deal to think about in the days after he saw the vision and before he entered Cornelius's house. Although he had physically walked and talked with Jesus, Peter's heart still needed to be converted to include a love of all people.

Cornelius was still at the beginning of the process. He didn't yet know of the good news, but we can see in the way Cornelius followed without hesitation the exact directions from the angel in his vision that he was more than ready to believe. Not only was his heart prepared, but Cornelius was humble enough to learn from Peter in spite of his own superior social position as a leader in the Roman army. Centurions commanded a hundred men in a legion, the equivalent of a company today, and were well respected in the communities where they were stationed. Cornelius's rank also made it unusual that he would follow the teachings of Judaism; Roman soldiers were expected to participate in emperor worship, which was part of the state religion of Rome. Like Peter, Cornelius had to reject a way of belief that he had previously understood in order to follow the leadings of God. That is why his attentiveness to what Peter taught and his subsequent conversion is so amazing. What an example for us.

Finally, we see that prayer, particularly listening, reflective prayer, is an essential discipline in the lives of those whose hearts have been converted to God. Peter went to the roof to pray, as we can imagine was his daily habit, and God spoke to him through a vision. We also see that prayer is a wonderful way to prepare our hearts for the Holy Spirit to work within. It cannot be a coincidence that Cornelius, who "prayed constantly to God" (10:2), was one of the first Gentiles to receive the good news and be filled with the Holy Spirit and baptized.

How was your heart prepared to accept Christ?

REFLECTION QUESTION
Allow each person a few moments to respond.

▶▶▶▶ POINTING TO GOD

As Ellen White wrote in the Devotional Reading, it is possible to profess a belief in Christ but still leave our hearts or a part of them untouched by God. Others of us may undergo a further conversion of the heart or an experience of God even after being Christian for many years. Such was the experience of John Wesley, the eighteenth-century Christian who is credited with founding Methodism. In 1725, as a young man attending Oxford University, Wesley dedicated himself to God. Although he cofounded the famous Holy Club, studied numerous religious texts, and was ordained as an Anglican priest, it wasn't until 1738 that Wesley

✍ Choose one member to read this section.

experienced what he called a strange warming of his heart by God. Perhaps the words of his journal tell the story best:

> Tuesday, 7 [February 1738]—(A day much to be remembered.) At the house of Mr. Weinantz, a Dutch merchant, I met Peter Böhler* [and others] just then landed from Germany.

> Saturday, 18 [February 1738]—I conversed much with Peter Böhler, but I understood him not; and least of all when he said, "My brother, my brother, that philosophy of yours must be purged away."

> Saturday, 22 [April 1738]—I met Peter Böhler once more. I had no objection to what he said of the nature of faith; but I could not understand how this faith should be given in a moment; how a man could *at once* be thus turned from darkness to light, from sin and misery to righteousness and joy in the Holy Ghost.

> Wednesday, 26 [April 1738]—P. Böhler walked with me a few miles and exhorted me not to stop short of the grace of God.

> Wednesday, 24 [May 1738]—In the evening I went very unwillingly to a society in Aldersgate Street, where one was reading Luther's preface to the Epistle to the Romans. About a quarter before nine, while he was describing the change which God works in the heart through faith in Christ, I felt my heart strangely warmed. I felt I did trust in Christ, Christ alone, for salvation; and an assurance was given me that He had taken away my sins, even mine, and saved me from the law of sin and death.[4]

▶▶▶▶ GOING FORWARD

Have another person read this section.

Converting the heart is one of the most difficult issues we face as Christians. All of us believe in the reality of God, and many of us have sophisticated theological knowledge. But it doesn't matter how theologically astute we are if we are unable to bring ourselves to a place where we are open to hearing and obeying God. Ellen White wrote that the great truth of the conversion of the heart is found in Jesus's words to Nicodemus: "No one can see the kingdom of God without being born from above," that is, born of the Spirit (John 3:3). It is the Spirit that enables a conversion of the heart, but we prepare ourselves to receive the Spirit, like Peter and Cornelius did, with Spiritual Disciplines such as prayer. Like Cornelius

* A Moravian missionary.

and John Wesley, we open ourselves to the teachings of those God places in our path. Then we commit ourselves to obeying the leadings of the Spirit, even when they take us down a path that contradicts what we previously understood. Then we do it all again. Our hearts can be converted over and over as we allow God to correct us and make us even more like Jesus Christ. This is the path of holiness, the way of discipleship.

When have you had a heart-warming experience of God?

REFLECTION QUESTION
Again, allow each member a few moments to answer this question.

This concludes our look at converting the heart. In the next chapter we will turn our attention to another avenue of living the mission—overcoming cultural captivity.

⊰ After everyone has had a chance to respond, the leader reads this paragraph.

CLOSING PRAYER

I will extol you, my God and King,
    and bless your name forever and ever.
Every day I will bless you,
    and praise your name forever and ever.
Great is the LORD, and greatly to be praised;
    his greatness is unsearchable.

One generation shall laud your works to another,
    and shall declare your mighty acts.
On the glorious splendor of your majesty,
    and on your wondrous works, I will meditate.
The might of your awesome deeds shall be proclaimed,
    And I will declare your greatness. (PS 145:1–6)

⊰ **Allow some time for members to encourage one another to read the Devotional and Scripture Readings and do the exercise in the following chapter before the next meeting.** Then invite the members to be silent for a few moments before leading them in reading the Closing Prayer aloud together.

⊰ At the end of the Closing Prayer, the leader asks for a volunteer to lead the next meeting.

TAKING IT FURTHER

The Scripture Reading implied that both Peter and Cornelius had a specific time set aside each day for prayer. If you do not have a scheduled daily prayer time, try setting aside a half hour at the same time each day this week for prayer. Many people find that morning is a good time to do this, but each person is different. Choose the time that you think will work best for you. In each prayer session be sure to ask God to help your heart remain open to him.

ADDITIONAL EXERCISE

ADDITIONAL RESOURCES

Foster, Richard J. *Celebration of Discipline*. San Francisco: HarperSanFrancisco, 1998.

White, Ellen G. "Genuine Conversion." *Advent Review and Sabbath Herald—1904*, no. 29, available at http://www.gilead.net.

Willard, Dallas. *Renovation of the Heart*. Colorado Springs, CO: NavPress, 2002.

ADDITIONAL REFLECTION QUESTIONS

In the exercise, we read that the Spiritual Disciplines are a God-given tool to prepare our hearts for God's transforming work. What disciplines from the list have been most helpful in your spiritual journey? Which have you yet to practice regularly?

Peter's vision showed him that he had to reevaluate his ideas about the way God worked in the world. What ideas have you had to change as you proceeded along the path of discipleship?

Like John Wesley, most of us have had several experiences of further conversion of the heart, or perhaps the mind, as we seek to follow God. What have been some of the most significant conversions or further experiences of God in your life?

OVERCOMING CULTURAL CAPTIVITY

KEY SCRIPTURE: Acts 15:1–19, 21

DEVOTIONAL READING

MARTIN LUTHER KING JR., "Letter from Birmingham Jail"

April 16, 1963

My Dear Fellow Clergymen:

While confined here in the Birmingham city jail, I came across your recent statement calling my present activities "unwise and untimely." Seldom do I pause to answer criticism of my work and ideas. If I sought to answer all the criticisms that cross my desk, my secretaries would have little time for anything other than such correspondence in the course of the day, and I would have no time for constructive work. But since I feel that you are men of genuine good will and that your criticisms are sincerely set forth, I want to try to answer your statements in what I hope will be patient and reasonable terms....

One of the basic points in your statement is that the action that I and my associates have taken in Birmingham is untimely. Some have asked: "Why didn't you give the new city administration time to act?"...

We know through painful experience that freedom is never voluntarily given by the oppressor; it must be demanded by the oppressed. Frankly, I have yet to engage in a direct-action campaign that was "well timed" in the view of those who have not suffered unduly from the disease of segregation. For years now I have heard the word "Wait!" It rings in the ear of every Negro with piercing familiarity. This "Wait" has almost always meant "Never." We must come to see, with one of our distinguished jurists, that "justice too long delayed is justice denied."

We have waited for more than 340 years for our constitutional and God-given rights. The nations of Asia and Africa are moving with jet-like speed toward gaining political independence, but we still creep at

It is helpful for everyone to read the Devotional and Scripture Readings and do the My Life with God Exercise before the meeting. Begin the meeting with silent prayer, then move directly to Reflecting on My Life with God below.

horse-and-buggy pace toward gaining a cup of coffee at a lunch counter. Perhaps it is easy for those who have never felt the stinging darts of segregation to say, "Wait." But when you have seen vicious mobs lynch your mothers and fathers at will and drown your sisters and brothers at whim; when you have seen hate-filled policemen curse, kick and even kill your black brothers and sisters; when you see the vast majority of your twenty million Negro brothers smothering in an airtight cage of poverty in the midst of an affluent society; when you suddenly find your tongue twisted and your speech stammering as you seek to explain to your six-year-old daughter why she can't go to the public amusement park that has just been advertised on television, and see tears welling up in her eyes when she is told that funtown is closed to colored children, and see ominous clouds of inferiority beginning to form in her little mental sky, and see her beginning to distort her personality by developing an unconscious bitterness toward white people; when you have to concoct an answer for a five-year-old son who is asking: "Daddy, why do white people treat colored people so mean?"; when you take a cross-country drive and find it necessary to sleep night after night in the uncomfortable corners of your automobile because no motel will accept you; when you are humiliated day in and day out by nagging signs reading "white" and "colored"; when your first name becomes "nigger," your middle name becomes "boy" (however old you are) and your last name becomes "John," and your wife and mother are never given the respected title "Mrs."; when you are harried by day and haunted by night by the fact that you are a Negro, living constantly at tiptoe stance, never quite knowing what to expect next, and are plagued with inner fears and outer resentments; when you are forever fighting a degenerating sense of "nobodiness" then you will understand why we find it difficult to wait. There comes a time when the cup of endurance runs over, and men are no longer willing to be plunged into the abyss of despair....

Oppressed people cannot remain oppressed forever. The yearning for freedom eventually manifests itself, and that is what has happened to the American Negro. Something within has reminded him of his birthright of freedom, and something without has reminded him that it can be gained....

Things are different now. So often the contemporary church is a weak, ineffectual voice with an uncertain sound. So often it is an archdefender of the status quo. Far from being disturbed by the presence of the church, the power structure of the average community is consoled by the church's silent and often even vocal sanction of things as they are.

But the judgment of God is upon the church as never before. If today's church does not recapture the sacrificial spirit of the early church, it will lose its authenticity, forfeit the loyalty of millions, and be dismissed as an irrelevant social club with no meaning for the twentieth century.... I hope the church as a whole will meet the challenge of this decisive hour.[1]

MY LIFE WITH GOD EXERCISE

All of us are captive to our culture in many ways we recognize, and in many ways we do not suspect. Martin Luther King Jr. wrote this famous letter in response to a letter from a group of white pastors who took issue with the tactics of nonviolent direct action he used to fight racial inequality. Because of the courageous work of King and many other figures in the civil rights movement, during the last fifty years our nation has focused a great deal of attention on correcting discriminatory practices and attitudes toward African-Americans, but prejudice is still a reality—not only for those who represent a minority in terms of ethnicity or religion, but also for the handicapped, women, the mentally retarded, those who are poor, uneducated, ill, obese, elderly, or single, and many others.

During your prayer times this week, first try to think of a time when you were discriminated against. Perhaps you were turned down for a job or were refused service or treated rudely at a store or restaurant because of your age or race or another physical characteristic. Maybe someone just made a hurtful comment about you. Think about how the incident or incidents made you feel. Consider how you reacted or wish you had reacted. Then try to place yourself in the position of the people who treated you that way. What do you think might have caused them to have such an attitude? Next, write down as many types of discrimination as you can think of. You might want to start with the above list. By each category list a person you know who fits that category and has been discriminated against or suffered for it. For example, a person in a wheelchair who perhaps cannot go to certain restaurants or functions because they are not accessible, or a female acquaintance who has suffered discrimination at the hands of her family or church or employer. And so on. As you are considering these matters, ask the Holy Spirit to help you identify the categories and people.

When you feel you have exhausted this part of the exercise, choose one person on your list to seek out in friendship or to help. Challenge yourself to choose a category that makes you uncomfortable, a person or group of people you perhaps have little experience with or recognize that you hold prejudices against. For example, offer to care for the mentally retarded person on your list for a couple of hours while his caretaker goes to the grocery store, or go with them on a walk. Visit an elderly person or take her on an errand. Go to a movie or eat dinner with a person of a different ethnicity or race. Pay attention to any feelings of uneasiness. These may run the gamut from feeling awkward and worrying about saying or doing the wrong thing to hoping that none of your friends see you to being concerned for your safety. Consider where such reactions might have come from and what misunderstandings or assumptions they might be based on. The best way to overcome such feelings is to face them head on by spending time with those about whom you may have learned discriminatory or prejudicial attitudes.

What did you learn about yourself and your cultural biases?

REFLECTING ON MY LIFE WITH GOD
Allow each member a few moments to answer this question.

After everyone has had a chance to respond to the question, ask a member to read this passage from Scripture.

► SCRIPTURE READING: ACTS 15:1–19, 21

Then certain individuals came down from Judea and were teaching the brothers, "Unless you are circumcised according to the custom of Moses, you cannot be saved." And after Paul and Barnabas had no small dissension and debate with them, Paul and Barnabas and some of the others were appointed to go up to Jerusalem to discuss this question with the apostles and the others. So they were sent on their way by the church, and as they passed through both Phoenicia and Samaria, they reported the conversion of the Gentiles, and brought great joy to all the believers. When they came to Jerusalem, they were welcomed by the church and the apostles and the elders, and they reported all that God had done with them. But some believers who belonged to the sect of the Pharisees stood up and said, "It is necessary for them to be circumcised and ordered to keep the law of Moses."

The apostles and the elders met together to consider this matter. After there had been much debate, Peter stood up and said to them, "My brothers, you know that in the early days God made a choice among you, that I should be the one through whom the Gentiles would hear the message of the good news and become believers. And God, who knows the human heart, testified to them by giving them the Holy Spirit, just as he did to us; and in cleansing their hearts by faith he has made no distinction between them and us. Now therefore why are you putting God to the test by placing on the neck of the disciples a yoke that neither our ancestors nor we have been able to bear? On the contrary, we believe that we will be saved through the grace of the Lord Jesus, just as they will."

The whole assembly kept silence, and listened to Barnabas and Paul as they told of the signs and wonders that God had done through them among the Gentiles. After they finished speaking, James replied, "My brothers, listen to me. Simeon has related how God first looked favorably on the Gentiles, to take from among them a people for his name. This agrees with the words of the prophets, as it is written,

> 'After this I will return,
> and I will rebuild the dwelling of David, which has fallen;
> from its ruins I will rebuild it, and I will set it up,
> so that all other peoples may seek the Lord—
> even all the Gentiles over whom my name has been called.
> Thus says the Lord, who has been making these
> things known from long ago.'

Therefore I have reached the decision that we should not trouble those Gentiles who are turning to God.... For in every city, for generations past, Moses has had those who proclaim him, for he has been read aloud every sabbath in the synagogues."

Try to put yourself in the position of the early Christians who were facing this question. What kind of things do you think they were struggling with as they debated the question of whether the Gentile converts needed to be circumcised or not?

REFLECTION QUESTION
Allow each person a few moments to respond to this question.

▶▶ GETTING THE PICTURE

After the Holy Spirit fell on Cornelius and his household, and Peter baptized them, he went to Jerusalem, where he was soundly criticized by those believers who had Jewish backgrounds. Peter recounted in detail what had happened—his vision, the three men sent by Cornelius to fetch him, his conversation with Cornelius upon their arrival—ending his summary with a description of the Holy Spirit's action, to which he added, "And I remembered the words of the Lord, how he had said, 'John baptized with water, but you will be baptized with the Holy Spirit.' If then God gave them the same gift that he gave us when we believed in the Lord Jesus Christ, who was I that I could hinder God?" (Acts

✑ After a brief discussion, choose one person to read this section.

11:16–17). This silenced Peter's critics, who agreed, "God has given even to the Gentiles the repentance that leads to life" (v 18).

Meanwhile, Barnabas and Saul, now known as Paul, were commissioned in the church at Antioch (the capital of Syria) and set off on what we now call the first missionary journey, traveling to places like Cyprus, Perga, and Attalia and preaching the word to Gentiles and Jews. When they returned to their home church at Antioch, "they called the church together and related all that God had done with them, and how he had opened a door of faith for the Gentiles" (14:27b).

These events lead to the dispute described in the Scripture Reading, between Judaizers—religious leaders who believed that a person had to be circumcised and be in obedience to the law of Moses before they could be saved—and those who had witnessed the Holy Spirit falling on Gentiles. It was hard for many to accept that God was moving among men before they had been circumcised and had committed themselves to the Mosaic law. But underneath there was much more going on. The Church was in danger of being captured by the culture, influenced by a cultural prejudice that had taken hold within the Jewish faith. After generations of wars with those around them and numerous foreign occupations, even a long exile, many Israelites held a deep-seated mistrust of people from other races and cultures. Abraham and his descendants were supposed to be a blessing for all people, but some believed Judaism and the Mosaic law were their race's private path to God and preferred not to share their faith with anyone outside their ethnic group. We see this tendency clearly exemplified in the story of Jonah, who balked at proclaiming God's message to the Ninevites because he did not want these enemies of Israel even to have the chance to repent. In contrast, the early Christians felt that it took the birth, life, death, and resurrection of Jesus Christ for God's promise to Abraham to become a reality. The council in Jerusalem was *the* critical watershed moment in the life of the Church that determined if it would be just another movement within Judaism or a faith that moved beyond cultural boundaries.

▶▶▶ GOING DEEPER

✍ Have another member read this section.

This event reveals several things about our spiritual heritage. First, even when we are sincerely convinced we are proclaiming the good news without adding anything, we must be careful. The Judaizers were convinced that those who believed in Christ must first become circumcised and practice the Mosaic law before they could be saved, but their beliefs were misplaced. They were so enmeshed in Judaism that they were unable to see that they were putting unnecessary burdens on non-Jewish converts. We have to be careful that we do not act similarly. When we demand that people do certain things at certain times, beyond what Jesus required to make them right with God, we are guilty of the same offense. Our church traditions, rituals, and practices certainly have value and powerful symbolism for us, but they can also be as big a trap as the traditions and practices of Judaism were for the Judaizers. Recognizing that a certain style of worship or prayer or of celebrating a sacrament is powerful for us because of familiarity or long tradition is one thing; requiring that all other believers follow exactly the same practice is quite another. Those of us who have been raised in only one church or denomination are especially prone to this captivity to tradition. Even though we may be tempted to hold firmly to our traditions, adding anything beyond what Jesus requires is risky business indeed.

There are times when a problem surpasses any one individual's ability to solve it. Cultural conflicts are particularly problematic because our cultural traditions are often so deeply ingrained that it is difficult for us to recognize and think about them without outside help. When the Judaizers arrived in Antioch with their teaching, Paul and Barnabas debated them. In spite of the apostles' skilled powers of persuasion, they were evidently unable to change the Judaizers' minds. To settle the issue, the Church sent Barnabas, Paul, and others to Jerusalem to present the problem to the apostles and elders. There is an important lesson here. Often we are too proud to admit that we need outside help to solve a problem; many a church has been destroyed over a conflict after failing to seek outside counsel. We find that even in Jerusalem, some members who were Pharisees believed it was necessary for Gentiles to be circumcised and obey the Mosaic law. It took the combined wisdom of the apostles and elders in Jerusalem, and particularly the resolve and insight of James, to solve the problem. Likewise, there are times in our fellowships when a problem is too big for our small group or our church or our synod to handle. This is when we go to our leaders for help and wisdom.

God, not us, decides who should come to faith in him. In Galatians Paul expresses much the same thought: "There is no longer Jew or Greek, there is no longer slave or free, there is no longer male and female; for all of you are one in Christ Jesus" (3:28). When we start thinking that we know who should enter God's kingdom, we are playing God. We are called to tell people the good news and make disciples, not decide whom God saves. That is God's business.

REFLECTION QUESTION
Allow each person a few
moments to respond.

How can we distinguish between what Jesus requires and those parts of our belief system that might be purely cultural? Can you think of any examples within your own church?

▶▶▶ POINTING TO GOD

Since the beginning of the Church, Christ's command to us to go and make disciples has led to difficult and challenging issues in the missionary field. Missionaries with the heartfelt desire to bring others to God have gone into the mission field and, often unconsciously, pressed their cultural preferences on their converts right along with the good news of the gospel, sometimes with devastating results. A prime example is the checkered history of the missionary efforts on Native American reservations in the United States. In the mid to late nineteenth century, missionaries from many denominations, including Presbyterian, Episcopalian, Methodist, and Catholic, flocked to the reservations, supported and funded by the government's "Civilization Fund," established in 1819.[2] The missionaries immediately founded schools, usually boarding schools. There was a practical reason for this—many families with school-age children lived too far from the mission to attend day school—but there was also a definite mandate from the government to acculturate the Native American children by separating them from their families. As a Bureau of Indian Affairs agent assigned to the Blackfeet wrote in 1875, "A boarding school is the only practical method in which to inculcate and ingress the minds of the coming generation with the superiority of civilized over the uncouth and precarious course of life in the wigwam."[3]

By 1884 missionary schools had been established in more than seventy-three tribes, and students totaled more than 239,000. The students were forced to speak English, a language unfamiliar to most of them, and were punished for speaking their native dialects. They were assigned new English names and told they had to cut their hair and dress like the whites around them, a dictate that many found confusing when they were told it was all in the name of the long-haired, robed or loinclothed Jesus depicted in the churches they were forced to attend. But far more devastating was the fact that entire generations who had been reared away from their families, in many cases only seeing them once or twice a year, lost the ability to speak their native languages and never learned their own cultural customs and traditions. The boarding schools effectively guaranteed that many native languages and traditions were lost forever.

Churches on the reservations have come a long way since these early boarding school days. Changes such as Vatican II have created much more openness to other religious traditions. Contemporary missionaries to the reservations still cope with the mistrust and rage of the peoples whose culture and traditions were co-opted or, in some cases—particularly that of the Lakota—almost obliterated by mostly well-meaning missionaries who were unable to distinguish between the good news of the gospel and their own cultural standards. Today those who pastor reservation churches often join in the cultural practices of the people. For example, Dan Smail and Joe Bailey, Lutheran ministers who staff a church on the Chippewa Cree reservation in Rocky Boy, Montana, join local residents several times a week in sweats, traditional ceremonies held in sweat lodges where participants pour water over heated rocks to produce steam. Sweat lodges are ubiquitous among North American Native Americans, but what takes place during a sweat varies widely from tribe to tribe and lodge to lodge, including everything from undirected conversation and relaxation to formal ceremonies. What started as a nod to cultural traditions has become an important part of the spiritual practice of the two ministers. Smail recites the Lord's Prayer and the Apostle's Creed and sings Lutheran hymns during the sweats. "It's a spiritual discipline—a time of serious prayer and communion with other people," he said. "Also, it's a form of respect. My faith is the same, but I feel more comfortable. In the sweat lodge, we pray more effortlessly."[4] Their admiration for and participation in Native American culture has paid off. When Bailey arrived on the reservation, his church had six members. Now it has one hundred.

▶▶▶▶▶ GOING FORWARD

All churches mix religious tradition with cultural tradition in one way or another. Look at the way various churches visually depict Jesus, the style of music played in different congregations, the diverse attire of religious leaders and congregations, just to name a few. What is dangerous is when we confuse the cultural preferences within our churches with mandatory requirements for every disciple. Our cultural understandings can be compared to a large iceberg. While a small part of the iceberg is visible above the surface, the vast majority of it lurks invisibly below. In the same way, most of our cultural assumptions are such a part of us that we may not even be able to identify them as cultural rather than universal until another culture's conflicting understanding or way of doing things bumps up against them.

Have another person read this section.

And this kind of challenge is usually a good thing. We should constantly ask ourselves how our Western way of doing and looking at things affects our lives and our ideas about God. Our focus on individualism, competition, material possessions—how are these things reflected in the way we live life, in what we believe about God and how we act upon that belief? It is here again that we make ourselves subject to the Holy Spirit, constantly and humbly asking for guidance and the continued understanding that our way of doing things is not necessarily God's way or even the best way and rejoicing once again that the kingdom of God is indeed open to all.

REFLECTION QUESTION
Again, allow each member a few moments to answer this question.

What kind of conflicts has your church had with "outsiders" who had a different interpretation of the rules or traditions of your denomination?

꙳ After everyone has had a chance to respond, the leader reads this paragraph.

꙳ **Allow some time for members to encourage one another to read the Devotional and Scripture Readings and do the exercise in the following chapter before the next meeting.** Then invite the members to be silent for a few moments before leading them in reading the Closing Prayer aloud together.

꙳ At the end of the Closing Prayer, the leader asks for a volunteer to lead the next meeting.

This concludes our look at overcoming cultural captivity. In the next chapter we will turn our attention to another avenue of living the mission—going global.

CLOSING PRAYER

I will extol you, my God and King,
    and bless your name forever and ever.
Every day I will bless you,
    and praise your name forever and ever.
Great is the LORD, and greatly to be praised;
    his greatness is unsearchable.

One generation shall laud your works to another,
    and shall declare your mighty acts.
On the glorious splendor of your majesty,
    and on your wondrous works, I will meditate.
The might of your awesome deeds shall be proclaimed,
    And I will declare your greatness. (PS 145:1–6)

TAKING IT FURTHER

ADDITIONAL EXERCISE

Look through the Yellow Pages or a local church directory and choose the church that you think is most unlike your own in terms of practice or belief and then attend a worship service there. Pay close attention to the differences and similarities in service, liturgy, music, and so on, between this church and your own. Spend some time considering which differences truly reflect theological understanding and which are culturally based.

Foster, Richard J. *Freedom of Simplicity*. Rev. ed. San Francisco: HarperSanFrancisco, 2005.

King, Martin Luther, Jr., "Letter from Birmingham Jail." Atlanta, GA: The Estate of Martin Luther King Jr., n.d. Available at http://www.thekingcenter.org.

Long, Thomas G. *Beyond the Worship Wars*. Herndon, VA: Alban Institute, 2001.

Tinker, George. *Missionary Conquest: The Gospel and Native American Cultural Genocide*. Minneapolis, MN: Augsburg Fortress, 1993.

ADDITIONAL RESOURCES

As controversial as the civil rights movement was at the time, certainly very few people today would disagree with King, Rosa Parks, and other proponents of rights for African-Americans. Do you see any contemporary movements within society in general that are controversial now but in the future may be viewed very differently?

ADDITIONAL REFLECTION QUESTIONS

How do you think you would react if your church service started to incorporate elements from other cultures—for example, mariachi music instead of a praise band or organ, songs sung in a Native American language, taking rice for communion as is sometimes done in Asia, or pictures of Jesus as an African? Which changes would be harder or easier for you to accept? Would such changes be positive for your church? Explain.

As honestly as you can, think about your own attitude toward "outsiders" in your church. If you were a disciple in the early Church, do you think you would have been on the side of the Judaizers or those who felt that Gentiles should be allowed to join their fellowship without being circumcised?

GOING GLOBAL

KEY SCRIPTURE: Acts 16:6–15

DEVOTIONAL READING

PAUL TOURNIER, *The Adventure of Living*

To his contemporaries Jesus was a true adventurer. His disciples were filled with such enthusiasm that they left everything to follow him in his extraordinary adventure.... While the common people admired in Jesus the adventurer who hits out at the injustices of society, for the same reason he drew down upon himself the hate of the cultured, the distinguished, and the religious people of his day. He was continually defying and scandalizing them.... Thus the adventure of the conflict unfolded relentlessly. Jesus accepted it and followed it to the end, as it came to a head in the drama of the Passion....

But God did not let go. He raised Jesus Christ and fortified his disciples, sending to them his Holy Spirit. Once more he chose a people—his Church. Entrusting his sacraments to it, he started it out on the great adventure of preaching the Gospel "to the end of the earth" (Acts 1:8). There follows the absorbing adventure of the book of the Acts of the Apostles, the wonderful adventure of St. Paul. The apostles proclaim to the Jews, and then to the Greeks, the decisive intervention of God in the world. Henceforward a meaning, a direction, and goal are given to the whole of history as well as to the life of each individual person. "Forgetting what lies behind and straining forward to what lies ahead, I press on toward the goal," wrote St. Paul (Philippians 3:13–14). That is indeed adventure!

The Christian churches today are seeking to recover the missionary outlook of the early pioneers. Until just a few years ago, missions meant only the sending of Gospel witnesses out to distant and pagan people. Now we realize that it involves a much more immediate and comprehensive adventure, affecting us all: the need to restore its soul to our so-called Christian (but profoundly de-Christianized) civilization.... In his

> ✐ It is helpful for everyone to read the Devotional and Scripture Readings and do the My Life with God Exercise before the meeting. Begin the meeting with silent prayer, then move directly to Reflecting on My Life with God below.

book *L'Annonce de l'Evangile Aujourd'hui*, Father J. Daniélou points out the distinction that should be made between the *Kerygma* (the "very first announcement of the Christian event") and catechesis, homily, or theology (the instruction of the faithful), to which preaching had hitherto been confined in countries that were within the Christian tradition. "The *Kerygma*," he writes, "has as its object the announcement of an event. It is the proclamation of something that is happening. This makes the *Kerygma* essentially different from instruction bearing on a theoretical doctrine." … The primitive missionary adventure which must be rediscovered now is the proclamation of the adventure of God in saving the world.[1]

MY LIFE WITH GOD EXERCISE

In the above excerpt, Paul Tournier, a twentieth-century Swiss doctor who wrote on topics of health and Christian faith, conveys a sense of the adventure that the first-generation Christians felt as they were proclaiming the good news of Jesus Christ throughout the countries rimming the Mediterranean Sea and beyond. Acknowledging that this excitement is no longer present in the contemporary church, he focuses not on what we traditionally understand as missions to people in faraway lands, but reminds us that our own Western culture is now a primary mission field. The adventure facing us all is to announce the Christian event to secularized people and groups that are, at best, indifferent and, at worst, hostile to the gospel of Jesus Christ.

As a part of your study time, read the book of Acts through at least once, noting the excitement, urgency, and sense of adventure expressed in the sermons and actions of the apostles and disciples. If you want, outline Acts as you are reading it. Do you find that reading about the early Church fills you with a sense of excitement and urgency about proclaiming the gospel? Does it suggest to you any ways you can proclaim the gospel to those in your community?

What ideas did you get about proclaiming the Christian event (Kerygma) *after reading through Acts?*

REFLECTING ON MY LIFE WITH GOD
Allow each member a few moments to answer this question.

After everyone has had a chance to respond to the question, ask a member to read this passage from Scripture.

► **SCRIPTURE READING:** ACTS 16:6–15

[Paul and Silas] went through the region of Phrygia and Galatia, having been forbidden by the Holy Spirit to speak the word in Asia. When they had come opposite Mysia, they attempted to go into Bithynia, but the Spirit of Jesus did not allow them; so, passing by Mysia, they went down to Troas. During the night Paul had a vision: there stood a man of Macedonia pleading with him and saying, "Come over to Macedonia and help us." When he had seen the vision, we immediately tried to cross over to Macedonia, being convinced that God had called us to proclaim the good news to them.

We set sail from Troas and took a straight course to Samothrace, the following day to Neapolis, and from there to Philippi, which is a leading city of the district of Macedonia and a Roman colony. We remained in this city for some days. On the sabbath day we went outside the gate by the river, where we supposed there was a place of prayer; and we sat down and spoke to the women who had gathered there. A certain woman named Lydia, a worshiper of God, was listening to us; she was from the city of Thyatira and a dealer in purple cloth. The Lord opened her heart to listen eagerly to what was said by Paul. When she and her household were baptized, she urged us, saying, "If you have judged me to be faithful to the Lord, come and stay at my home."

What lessons do you take away from this passage about proclaiming the gospel?

REFLECTION QUESTION
Allow each person a few moments to respond to this question.

▶▶ GETTING THE PICTURE

In the Scripture Reading Paul is on yet another of his missionary journeys, this time with Silas. After spending some time at the church at Antioch, Paul is now ready to continue in his role of bringing the gospel to the Gentiles. William Barclay writes, "Paul was a born adventurer and could never stay long in the one place."[2] He begins by visiting churches he has already established in Asia Minor, present-day Turkey, and then ventures into the new territories mentioned in the Scripture Reading, Galatia and Phrygia. There Paul has the vision of the Macedonian man.

After a brief discussion, choose one person to read this section.

Macedonia, a region north of Greece, was perhaps a surprising place for Paul and his companion to want to preach the gospel, since it had a large population of Romans, who were generally distrusted by Jews. And the initial reaction there is perhaps predictable; despite the vision, Paul and Silas do not seem to be welcomed. They remain in Philippi for some days with no recorded results. When arriving in a new town, Paul's usual practice was to go to the local synagogue on the Sabbath and proclaim the gospel, but since Philippi contained no synagogue he searches out another place of prayer. In the small group of women gathered by the river Paul finds an attentive audience.

Although women had been disciples from the beginning, this is the only time we see Paul preaching exclusively to a group of women. This was partly because of the locale: women in Macedonia generally enjoyed more freedoms than Jewish or Roman women. Lydia, the Gentile "worshiper of God," is a prime example. While Roman women were confined to their homes, Lydia is free to worship at the river, where Paul is able to speak to her and the other women. She also runs her own business and invites Paul and Silas to stay at her home. These details and the fact that Lydia is named indicate her high status.

One interesting thing about our Scripture Reading: there is a change in personal pronouns between verses 6 and 10. In verse 6, Luke writes in the third person, "They went through," but in verse 10, he writes in the first person, "We immediately tried to cross over." Why the change? Barclay suggests that Paul was forbidden to go to new cities in Asia Minor because he was ill, prompting Luke, a doctor, to join the party at one of the cities Paul was revisiting and accompany him as far as Philippi (see 16:10–13, 15–17).[3]

▶▶▶ GOING DEEPER

✍ Have another member read this section.

Perhaps the most important principle we learn from the Scripture passage is that the good news is to be proclaimed throughout the world; it is a global message. In other words, the kingdom of God is not only available to non-Jews, it is not confined to one geographic area. Before the man from Macedonia appeared in his dream, Paul had confined his travels to the Middle Eastern region we know today as Jordan, Syria, and Turkey. Macedonia is in Europe. When Paul and those with him crossed the Adriatic Sea and landed in Europe, they opened up the world to the message of Jesus Christ, confirming Jesus's words, "Then he opened their minds to understand the scriptures, and he said to them, 'Thus it is written, that the Messiah is to suffer and to rise from the dead on the third day, and that repentance and forgiveness of sins is to be proclaimed in his name to all nations, beginning from Jerusalem. You are witnesses of these things'" (Luke 24:45–48).

We also learn that the Church continued to try to escape from cultural captivity. The council in Jerusalem broke down the walls between Jews and Gentiles. Paul's arrival in Macedonia started breaking down the barriers between the ethnic groups of the Middle East and Europe. When Paul "spoke to the women who had gathered there," the barrier of gender was shattered. Erasing the lines between Jew and Gentile, circumcised and uncircumcised, cultured and barbarian, male and female, slave and free in the Church defined the rest of Paul's life (see Gal 3:28; Col 3:11).

Though there was not a synagogue in Philippi, Paul stuck with a missionary strategy that worked. On the Sabbath he went "outside the gate by the river," where there was a place of prayer. This is exactly the same method Jesus used throughout his life: time after time he proclaimed the kingdom of God in the places where believers gathered—the temple and synagogue. In fact, the word *synagogue* is Greek for "gathering of things" or "assembly of people." By going to the temple and synagogue, or wherever people gathered for prayer on the Sabbath, both Jesus and Paul found a ready-made audience for their teaching. So we learn from Jesus and his followers that once we find a missionary strategy that works in a particular culture, we should keep to it.

Last, we learn that God honors obedience. It would have been easy for Paul to have ignored the Holy Spirit and instead gone to proclaim Jesus Christ in the synagogues of Asia. He chose differently, however, and as a consequence God the Holy Spirit made the heart of Lydia sensitive to what Paul said, which opened up a whole continent. Being obedient to the call of God is perhaps one of the hardest issues that we face. We are often unsure about what the Holy Spirit is prompting us to do. Unfortunately, many of us do not have the clarity of a dream to guide us; we have only internal promptings, which are easy to ignore or doubt. But with persistence and patience, we can become more sensitive to what God is asking of us so that we can do what needs to be done when it needs to be done.

How well are you able to hear and trust the internal promptings of the Holy Spirit?

REFLECTION QUESTION
Allow each person a few moments to respond.

>>>> **POINTING TO GOD**

The historical figure who has perhaps done the most since Paul to further the spread of Christianity across the globe is the early fourth-century Roman emperor Constantine. Constantine made Christianity a legal religion of the Roman Empire during his reign. When he first succeeded his father as ruler, or Caesar, in 306, Constantine ruled over a portion of the Roman Empire that included modern-day Britain, the Germanic provinces, Spain, and Gaul. He was constantly defending his territory against neighboring rulers and fellow claimants to the Roman throne. At the time, Christians were harshly persecuted by the other rulers of the empire, but Constantine saw in a vision that he would conquer with

✍ Choose one member to read this section.

the sign of Christ.[4] When he marched against rival emperor Maxentius, Constantine and his troops (although neither he nor most of them were actually Christians at the time) put Christ's monogram on their shields and soundly defeated Maxentius, even though Constantine's troops are believed to have been outnumbered 100,000 to 20,000.[5]

In gratitude for his victory, in 313 Constantine issued the Edict of Milan, which made Christianity legal throughout the entire Roman Empire, and persuaded the eastern Roman emperor, Licinius, to accept the edict. The importance of this legislation can hardly be overstated; it was a complete change for many Christians in the Roman empire. Those in prison were freed, and congregations were once again able to hold public services and build churches. Constantine made further concessions to the churches, allowing them to inherit property and exempting them from taxation. It bears mentioning that Christians were in the minority in most parts of the Roman Empire, making up a fifth of the western part and half of the eastern part.[6] This makes Constantine's decisions all the more remarkable. After ten years of peaceful coexistence, however, Licinius returned to persecuting Christians and threatened Constantine's position. Constantine defeated Licinius, becoming sole emperor of the Roman empire, a position he retained until his death in 337.

Constantine is a complex historical figure. Although many refer to him as the first Christian emperor, scholars debate whether he deserves that title. Though he actively supported the Church and worshiped among Christians, he also supported pagan worship throughout his reign and was only baptized on his deathbed. Many contend that under Constantine Christianity became a religion of the sword. Still others, such as Jacques Ellul in *The Subversion of Christianity,* see Constantine's act of legalizing Christianity as more negative than positive in Christian history. He argues that once the Church became supported by the state, its focus on loving God and loving neighbor was largely replaced with issues of liturgy, doctrine, and administration. Everyone does agree, however, that Constantine's actions represent a defining moment in the history of Christianity.

▶▶▶▶▶ GOING FORWARD

Have another person read this section.

It is hard to grasp the significance of these early events in Christian history—Paul crossing the Adriatic Sea to Macedonia and Constantine signing the Edict of Milan to make Christianity a religion that was no longer subject to persecution—but these two events contributed a great deal to the fact that those of us reading this book are likely Christians living in countries where Christianity is the majority religion or at least tolerated by the government. We can credit both events to the Holy Spirit. We know that Paul followed the urgings of the Spirit in his travels, and although we can't say for certain, it does seem that Constantine's vision came from the Spirit as well. How amazing to recognize that the Holy Spirit translates the gospel for all cultures, and that we can have a role in this great process of *Kerygma*.

Of course, as Tournier explains, we don't necessarily have to travel to faraway places or, like Constantine, be in a position to issue important edicts in order to proclaim the gospel. There are opportunities for us every day right where we live—to announce the good news, to model the good news, to live with the joy of the Holy Spirit and to rediscover the sense of adventure of God saving the world through the birth, life, death, and resurrection of Jesus Christ.

Like Peter, like Stephen, like Paul, we too are called to live the mission.

What does living the mission mean to you?

CLOSING PRAYER

I will extol you, my God and King,
    and bless your name forever and ever.
Every day I will bless you,
    and praise your name forever and ever.
Great is the LORD, and greatly to be praised;
    his greatness is unsearchable.

One generation shall laud your works to another,
    and shall declare your mighty acts.
On the glorious splendor of your majesty,
    and on your wondrous works, I will meditate.
The might of your awesome deeds shall be proclaimed,
    And I will declare your greatness. (PS 145:1–6)

TAKING IT FURTHER

Make a copy of the Devotional Reading for this chapter and give it to your pastor, asking if you can make an appointment with her or him to discuss

REFLECTION QUESTION
Again, allow each member a few moments to answer this question.

🕊 **After everyone has had a chance to respond, remind them that this is the last lesson in the book and ask the group if they would like to continue meeting together.** If everyone agrees they would like to continue, this would be a good time to discuss when they want to meet and what material to use.

🕊 When everyone has shared, the leader asks the members to be silent for a few moments before leading them in reading the Closing Prayer aloud together.

ADDITIONAL EXERCISE

it. In the course of your discussion, try to discern if your minister agrees or disagrees with Tournier's premise. If he or she agrees, ask how you can help to proclaim Jesus Christ to your community—pray for your church, pray for those who are proclaiming the *Kerygma,* go with your pastor to make calls on people in the community who have no church home. Should your pastor not agree with Tournier, listen to what he or she has to say about the topic and pray together for discernment for both of you.

ADDITIONAL RESOURCES

Jacques Ellul. *The Subversion of Christianity.* Grand Rapids, MI: Eerdmans, 1986.
Paul Tournier. *The Adventure of Living.* New York: Harper & Row, 1965.

ADDITIONAL REFLECTION QUESTIONS

In what ways are you most comfortable proclaiming the gospel?

What do you see as the most important aspect of mission work today?

We mentioned in the Going Deeper section that Paul's habit of stopping where people were gathered was a missionary strategy that worked. Do you have a tried-and-true missionary strategy? If so, what is it? If not, what do you think might work best in your personal mission field (your town, workplace, school, etc.)?

How do you perceive Constantine—as the first great Christian emperor, as a sinner who wrongly connected Christianity with the sword, as a person who subverted Christianity by making it a bureaucratic religion of the rulers? What do you think might have happened if Constantine hadn't legalized Christianity?

NOTES

�֎

CHAPTER 1: RECEIVING THE COMMISSION

1. Dallas Willard, *The Great Omission* (San Francisco: HarperSanFrancisco, 2006), 4–8.
2. Oswald Chambers, *My Utmost for His Highest* (New York: Dodd, Mead, 1935), 301.
3. Dallas Willard, *The Divine Conspiracy* (San Francisco: HarperSanFrancisco, 1998), 271.
4. Willard, *The Great Omission*, 7.
5. Willard, *The Divine Conspiracy*, 187.
6. John Wesley, *The Journal of John Wesley* (Grand Rapids, MI: Christian Classics Ethereal Library, n.d.), 183. Available at http://www.ccel.org.
7. "The Life of St. Ignatius Loyola." Available at http://www.luc.edu/jesuit/ignatius.bio.html.
8. Willard, *The Divine Conspiracy*, 293.

CHAPTER 2: BEING EMPOWERED BY THE SPIRIT

1. Billy Graham, *The Holy Spirit* (Waco, TX: Word, 1978), 28–30, 32, 35–36, 132–34.
2. John R. W. Stott, *Baptism and Fullness: The Work of the Holy Spirit Today* (Downers Grove, IL: InterVarsity, 1975), 27.
3. Stott, *Baptism and Fullness*, 30.
4. Gary B. McGee, "William Seymour and the Azusa Street Revival," *Enrichment Journal*. Available at http://www.ag.org/enrichmentjournal/199904/026_azusa.cfm.
5. Walter J. Hollenweger, *Pentecostalism: Origins and Developments Worldwide* (Peabody, MA: Hendrickson, 1997), 23.
6. McGee, "William Seymour."
7. Stott, *Baptism and Fullness*, 74–75.

CHAPTER 3: FORMING A COMMUNITY

1. Jean Vanier, *Community and Growth*, rev. ed. (New York: Paulist, 1989), 16–17, 18.
2. Richard J. Foster and others, eds., *The Renovaré Spiritual Formation Bible* (San Francisco: HarperSanFrancisco, 2005), 7.
3. Many of the ideas for this discussion are borrowed from a series of talks on the book of Acts by Dallas Willard at Woodlake Avenue Friends Church, Canoga Park, CA, 1972.
4. "Jean Vanier: A Biographical Sketch." Available at http://www.larchecanada.org/vanbio1.htm.
5. "Welcome to L'Arche." Available at http://www.larche.ca/en/home/welcome/.
6. Henri J. M. Nouwen, *The Road to Daybreak* (New York: Image, 1988), 98.
7. Eugene H. Peterson, *Christ Plays in Ten Thousand Places* (Grand Rapids, MI: Eerdmans, 2005), 226.

CHAPTER 4: PREACHING THE GOOD NEWS

1. Bruce Larson, *Wind and Fire* (Waco, TX: Word, 1984), 42–48.
2. James F. White, *The History of Christian Worship* (Nashville, TN: Abingdon, 1993), 35.

3. Philip Schaff, "Chrysostom as a Preacher," in *Saint Chrysostom: On the Priesthood; Ascetic Treatises; Select Homilies and Letter; Homilies on the Statutes* (Edinburgh: T&T Clark, 1886). Available at http://www.ccel.org.
4. Schaff, "Chrysostom as a Preacher."

CHAPTER 5: BEING THE GOOD NEWS

1. Adomnán of Iona, *Life of St Columba,* trans. Richard Sharpe (New York: Penguin, 1995), 156–58.
2. Bill Samuel, "Elizabeth Gurney Fry (1780–1845): Quaker Prison Reformer." Available at http://www.quakerinfo.com/fry.shtml.

CHAPTER 6: CHOOSING LEADERS

1. Robert K. Greenleaf, *Servant Leadership* (New York: Paulist, 1977), 7–8, 13–14.
2. Greg Roers, ed., *Eugene Friends Newsletter* (Feb. 2000), 6. Available at http://www.co-intelligence.org/P-Quakerbusiness.html.
3. Interview with Sharon Miner, *Amarillo Uptown* (Aug. 2006), 14.

CHAPTER 7: MAKING DISCIPLES

1. Max Lucado, *Just Like Jesus* (Nashville, TN: Word, 1998), 1–3.
2. Dallas Willard, *The Divine Conspiracy,* 282.
3. From *The Power of the Spirit*, cited by Richard J. Foster in RENOVARÉ *Perspective* (Vol. 15, No. 3, October 2005), 1.
4. G. Cyprian Alston, *The Rule of St. Benedict.* Available at http://www.newadvent.org/cathen/02436a.htm.
5. Kathleen Norris, *The Cloister Walk* (New York: Riverhead, 1996), 7.
6. Huston Smith, "Reasons for Joy," *Christian Century,* Oct. 4, 2005, 10.

CHAPTER 8: EXPERIENCING PERSECUTION

1. J. C. Robertson, "Tertullian, Perpetua and Companions (A.D. 181–206)," in *Sketches of Church History, from AD 33 to the Reformation* (New York: Gorham, 1904), 17. Available at http://www.ccel.org.
2. Many of the ideas contained in this section are borrowed from a series of talks on the book of Acts by Dallas Willard at Woodlake Avenue Friends Church, Canoga Park, CA, 1972.
3. John C. Raines, "Righteous Resistance and Martin Luther King, Jr.," *Christian Century,* January 18, 1984, 52. Available at http://www.religion-online.org/showarticle.asp?title=1365.
4. Martin Luther King Jr., "Letter from Birmingham Jail" (Atlanta, GA: The Estate of Martin Luther King Jr.). Available at http://www.thekingcenter.org.
5. King Jr., "Letter from Birmingham Jail."
6. King Jr., "Letter from Birmingham Jail."

CHAPTER 9: CONVERTING THE MIND

1. Alister McGrath, "God as My Guide," *Science & Spirit Magazine* 16, no. 04 (July/August 2005): 51–53.
2. McGrath, "God as My Guide."
3. Leo Tolstoy, *Confession* (Grand Rapids, MI: Christian Classics Ethereal Library, 1882), 8. Available at http://www.ccel.org.
4. Leo Tolstoy, *A Confession and Other Religious Writings,* trans. Jane Kentish (London: Penguin, 1988), 1.

CHAPTER 10: CONVERTING THE HEART

1. Ellen G. White, "Genuine Conversion," *Advent Review and Sabbath Herald-1904*, no. 29. Available at http://www.gilead.net.
2. Richard J. Foster, *Celebration of Discipline* (San Francisco: HarperSanFrancisco, 1998), 6, 7.
3. John R. W. Stott, *The Message of Acts* (Downers Grove, IL: InterVarsity Press, 1990), 185.
4. *Journal of John Wesley,* available at http://www.ccel.org/ccel/wesley/journal.titlepage.html.

CHAPTER 11: OVERCOMING CULTURAL CAPTIVITY

1. Martin Luther King Jr., "Letter from Birmingham Jail" (Atlanta, GA: The Estate of Martin Luther King Jr., n.d.). Available at http://www.thekingcenter.org.
2. Jana Noel, "Education Toward Cultural Shame: A Century of Native American Education," *Educational Foundations* (Winter 2002). Available at http://findarticles.com/p/articles/mi_qa3971/is_200201/ai_n9063054.
3. Noel, "Education Toward Cultural Shame."
4. Julia Roller, "Ministers in Montana," in *Native and Christian: A Look at Christianity on Indian Reservations* (Berkeley, CA: University of California Berkeley Graduate School of Journalism Web Site, 2000). Available at http://journalism.berkeley.edu/projects/nm/julia/ministers.html.

CHAPTER 12: GOING GLOBAL

1. Paul Tournier, *The Adventure of Living,* trans. Edwin Hudson (New York: Harper & Row, 1965), 78–81.
2. William Barclay, *The Acts of the Apostles,* rev. ed. (Philadelphia: Westminster, 1976), 118.
3. Barclay, *The Acts of the Apostles,* 121.
4. Charles G. Herbermann and George Grupp, "Constantine the Great," *New Advent Catholic Encyclopedia.* Available at http://www.newadvent.org/cathen/04295c.htm.
5. Herbermann and Grupp, "Constantine the Great."
6. Herbermann and Grupp, "Constantine the Great."

ABOUT THE AUTHORS

❖

Richard J. Foster is the founder of RENOVARÉ; author of six books, including *Celebration of Discipline, PRAYER: Finding the Heart's True Home*, and *Streams of Living Water*; and Editor of *The Renovaré Spiritual Formation Bible*, all of which effectively promote personal spiritual renewal. From his base near Denver, Colorado, Richard travels throughout the world, speaking and teaching on the spiritual life.

Lynda L. Graybeal has worked as Richard Foster's personal assistant for over two decades and was the Administrator/Editor of RENOVARÉ until 2004. She has written articles for the RENOVARÉ *Perspective* and appendices in *Streams of Living Water*, and was a General Editor of *The Renovaré Spiritual Formation Bible*. She lives in Canyon, Texas.

Julia L. Roller is a freelance writer and editor, was the project editor for *The Renovaré Spiritual Formation Bible*, and has written for publications such as *Group Magazine, Rev!, Children's Ministry, Go Deeper Retreats*, and *Young Adult Ministry in the 21st Century*. She lives in Coronado, California.

ACKNOWLEDGMENTS

❖

The seeds of this book lie in the rich material found in *The Renovaré Spiritual Formation Bible,* so first we must acknowledge and thank the other editors of that project—Richard J. Foster, Gayle Beebe, Thomas C. Oden, and Dallas Willard. Lyle SmithGraybeal has greatly enriched this guide with both his enthusiastic wellspring of ideas and his patient editing. At HarperOne Cynthia DiTiberio has also done a wonderful job with the editing of the manuscript. Michael G. Maudlin of HarperOne, Richard J. Foster and Lyle SmithGraybeal from Renovaré, and Kathryn Helmers of Helmers Literary Services first envisioned this series of spiritual formation guides, so we thank them for their support and encouragement as well as for the faith they had in us. Finally, we are especially grateful to our families, particularly our spouses, Phil Graybeal and Ryan Waterman, for their support, inspiration, and love.

Lynda L. Graybeal and Julia L. Roller

Grateful acknowledgment is made to the following for permission to reprint material copyrighted or controlled by them.

The Scripture quotations contained herein are from the *New Revised Standard Version Bible.* Copyright © 1989, 1993, by the Division of Christian Education of the National Council of the Churches of Christ in the United States of America. Used by permission. All rights reserved.

Excerpts from and adaptation of "The With-God Life: A General Introduction" from *The Renovaré Spiritual Formation Bible* by Renovaré and edited by Richard J. Foster. Copyright © 2005 by Renovaré, Inc. Used with permission of HarperCollins Publishers, 10 East 53rd Street, New York, NY, 10022-5299, www.harpercollins.com.

WHAT IS RENOVARÉ?

❖

RENOVARÉ (from the Latin meaning "to renew") is an infrachurch movement committed to the renewal of the Church of Jesus Christ in all its multifaceted expressions. Founded by best-selling author Richard J. Foster, RENOVARÉ is Christian in commitment, international in scope, and ecumenical in breadth.

In *The Renovaré Spiritual Formation Bible,* we observe how God spiritually formed his people through historical events and the practice of Spiritual Disciplines that is The With-God Life. RENOVARÉ continues this emphasis on spiritual formation by placing it within the context of the two-thousand-year history of the Church and six great Christian traditions we find in its life—Contemplative: The Prayer-Filled Life; Holiness: The Virtuous Life; Charismatic: The Spirit-Empowered Life; Social Justice: The Compassionate Life; Evangelical: The Word-Centered Life; and Incarnational: The Sacramental Life. This balanced vision of Christian faith and witness was modeled for us by Jesus Christ and was evident in the lives of countless saints: Antony, Francis of Assisi, Susanna Wesley, Phoebe Palmer, and others. The With-God Life of the People of God continues on today as Christians participate in the life and practices of local churches and look forward to spending eternity in that "all-inclusive community of loving persons with God himself at the very center of this community as its prime Sustainer and most glorious Inhabitant."

In addition to offering a balanced vision of the spiritual life, RENOVARÉ promotes a practical strategy for people seeking renewal by helping facilitate small spiritual formation groups; national, regional, and local conferences; one-day seminars; personal and group retreats; and readings from devotional classics that can sustain a long-term commitment to renewal. RENOVARÉ Resources for Spiritual Renewal, Spiritual Formation Guides, and *The Renovaré Spiritual Formation Bible*—books published by HarperSanFrancisco—seek to integrate historical, scholarly, and inspirational materials into practical, readable formats. These resources can be used in a variety of settings, including small groups, private and organizational retreats, individual devotions, and church school classes. Written and edited by people committed to the renewal of the Church, all of the materials present a balanced vision of Christian life and faith coupled with a practical strategy for spiritual growth and enrichment.

For more information about RENOVARÉ and its mission, please log on to its Web site (www.renovare.org) or write RENOVARÉ, 8 Inverness Drive East, Suite 102, Englewood, CO 80112-5624, USA.

Introducing a guide to deepening your spirituality

Combining the depth of a study Bible with the warmth of a devotional Bible, this revolutionary resource will make Scripture come alive in your daily life.

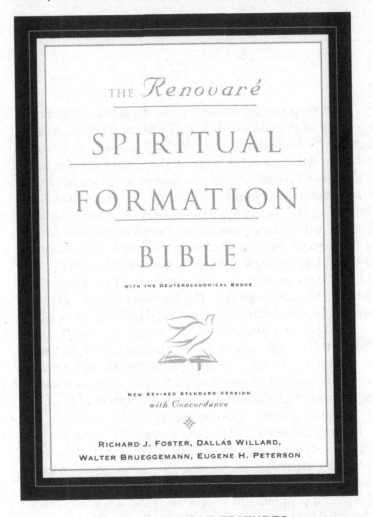

THIS UNIQUE BIBLE FEATURES:

The New Revised Standard Version • Fifteen progressive essays on living the "with-God life" • Introductions and notes for each book of the Bible, highlighting issues of spiritual formation and growth • Spiritual exercises • Profiles of key biblical characters • An Index that provides Bible references for each Spiritual Discipline • A Spiritual Formation Bibliography • Suggested Ways to Use This Bible for Spiritual Formation

0–06–067107–6 • $39.95/$51.50 (Can.)
0–06–067106–8 • $44.95/$56.50 (Can.)
with the Deuterocanonical Books

For more information on our books and authors visit www.authortracker.com.